Praise for *10 Excellent Reasons for National Health Care*

This book is *the* user's manual for those who will play an integral role in reversing the downward trends in the quality, access, and affordability of health care. In *10 Excellent Reasons for National Health* Care, some of the most notable leaders of this movement make it clear why support for H.R. 676 is ballooning all across the nation.
 —U.S. Representative Dennis J. Kucinich

Here is a lit stick of dynamite tossed into a discussion where explosives are desperately needed. There are far more than 10 excellent reasons why millions of Americans desperately need this book. It should become to the struggle to obtain universal national health care in the U.S. what *Uncle Tom's Cabin* was to the abolition movement.
 —Dave Marsh, activist, critic, and author

The evidence that our current health system is in deep trouble and not viable continues to mount. Whether we examine access, cost, or quality in our system, we are in serious trouble. *10 Excellent Reasons for National Health Care* is a clear, concise, and science-based analysis of the logic and benefits of national health care.
 —David Satcher, MD, PhD, and 16th U.S. Surgeon General

Good things come in ⸻ *Excellent Reasons for l* ⸻ imony on how to cure ⸻ uy many, and spread th ⸻
 —Elaine B⸻ Worklife
  Program,

This book addresses all questions about health care reform. Medicare for all is a right worth fighting for!
—Byllye Avery, founder, Avery Institute for Social Change

This little book does a great job of describing our embarrassing U.S. health care system that spends more money per capita on health care than any other country in the world and yet leaves 47 million people uninsured. It also points to a solution.
—Dr. Allan Rosenfield, Dean Emeritus, Mailman School of Public Health, Columbia University

The contributors to this highly readable book provide compelling reasons why the U.S. needs a national health care system similar to the ones that serve every industrialized country but ours at far less cost. Replacing our dysfunctional profit-making health insurance system with a universal-coverage single-payer system like Medicare will permit access to good medical care for all of us.
—Victor W. Sidel, MD, Professor of Social Medicine at Montefiore Medical Center and the Albert Einstein College of Medicine and past president of the American Public Health Association

Any worthwhile reform of our medical care system must include some type of "single-payer" insurance plan. This very readable collection of essays explains why. I recommend it highly.
—Arnold S. Relman, MD, former editor of the *New England Journal of Medicine*, Professor Emeritus of Medicine and of Social Medicine at Harvard Medical School, and author of *A Second Opinion: Rescuing America's Health Care*

10

Excellent Reasons for National Health Care

Edited by Mary E. O'Brien, MD
and Martha Livingston, PhD

THE NEW PRESS

NEW YORK
LONDON

Requests for permission to reproduce selections from this book should
be mailed to: Permissions Department, The New Press, 38 Greene Street,
New York, NY 10013.

Published in the United States by The New Press, New York, 2008
Distributed by W. W. Norton & Company, Inc., New York

ISBN 978-1-59558-328-4 (pb)
CIP data available

The New Press was established in 1990 as a not-for-profit alternative to
the large, commercial publishing houses currently dominating the book
publishing industry. The New Press operates in the public interest rather
than for private gain, and is committed to publishing, in innovative ways,
works of educational, cultural, and community value that are often
deemed insufficiently profitable.

www.thenewpress.com

Composition by Westchester Book Group

Printed in Canada

2   4   6   8   10   9   7   5   3

"Of all the forms of inequality, injustice in health care is the most shocking and inhumane."

—Martin Luther King Jr.

Contents

Foreword

Representative John Conyers Jr.

America faces a health care crisis that must be addressed now by Congress and the president. With 47 million uninsured Americans and another 50 million who are underinsured, it is past time to change our fragmented, inefficient, and costly nonsystem of health care.

This insightful book will provide you with the information you need to be an informed participant in the public debate about how to achieve health care for all. This information is especially important now, during this election year. Every candidate is talking about health care. Some are placing the blame for the health care crisis on the American people, arguing that our lifestyle and behavior are to blame for rising health care costs. Some would like to see the burden of rapidly escalating health care costs shifted away from employers and onto working Americans. Nearly all promote plans that will never get our health care costs under control or

Representative John Conyers Jr. is a 43-year member of the U.S. House of Representatives, the chairman of the House Committee on the Judiciary and the primary author of HR676, The United States Health Insurance Act.

guarantee all of us the health care we need, because these plans maintain the central role of the wasteful for-profit insurance companies.

Conservative health care reformers talk about maintaining "choice" in the American health care system. The truth is, most Americans have very little choice in health care today. If they can't afford insurance coverage, their choices are limited to paying for needed health care versus paying for other priorities like rent or groceries—always with the specter of debt or bankruptcy on the horizon. If they are very lucky, their employer may offer them a choice among a few insurance plans. However, among the shrinking number of Americans who still have employer-provided coverage, most only have the choice of accepting the insurance plan their employer offers or going without coverage. Once insured, choices are limited to whatever the insurance company wants to cover, consistent with its bottom line.

True universal health care means that all of us will have the choice of doctor, hospital, or caregiver, not merely a choice among insurance plans. And we will never have to choose between paying for health care and risking bankruptcy versus going without care. That's the goal of HR 676, the United States National Health Insurance Act. This uniquely American health insurance program with single-payer financing will ensure that everyone in this country, regardless of income, employment, race, or health status, has access to the highest-quality and most-cost-effective health care services. The bill would establish a publicly financed, privately delivered health care system that improves and expands the already existing Medicare program.

Within the chapters of this book and in the resource guide at the back, you will find cutting-edge information to help you work toward the only sensible solution to our health care crisis: a single-payer national health insurance program. Contributors to this book include doctors, nurses, patients, and an international union leader. They explain why health care is a human right. They discuss the benefits of a single-payer plan: that it is cost-effective; will provide choice, quality, and better health for Americans; will help to reduce health care disparities; will make doctors and nurses better able to do their jobs; and will benefit both workers and businesses. They will also explain why single-payer universal health care is the only approach that can guarantee Americans the health care they need when they need it and explain how, by working together, we can achieve the goal of health care for all.

I urge you to read this groundbreaking book and to get involved in the growing movement for single-payer health care!

John Conyers Jr.
Member of Congress
February 2008

10
Excellent Reasons
for National Health Care

THIS MODERN WORLD

THIS WEEK: STANDARD CONSERVATIVE RESPONSES TO HEALTH CARE REFORM!

1. FALSE EQUIVALENCY

THESE MODEST DEMOCRATIC PROPOSALS ARE THE *EXACT SAME THING AS SOCIALIZED MEDICINE!*

HOPE YOU KNOW THE WORDS TO THE "INTERNATIONALE," COMRADE!

2. FACILE JUXTAPOSITION

HEALTH CARE ISN'T VERY EXPENSIVE--AT LEAST WHEN COMPARED TO THINGS THAT ARE *MORE* EXPENSIVE!

LIKE HUGE TRUCK-LOADS OF *DIAMONDS!*

OR SWIMMING POOLS FULL OF *CAVIAR!*

5. SPECIOUS REBUTTALS

WHY STOP WITH HEALTH CARE? WHY NOT THROW IN GUARANTEED *CADILLACS* WHILE WE'RE AT IT?

DON'T I HAVE A "RIGHT" TO DRIVE A NICE CAR, MIS-TER LIBERAL? *HMMMM?*

6. FREE MARKET TRIUMPHALISM

PEOPLE SHOULD *SHOP AROUND* FOR HEALTH CARE, LIKE ANY *OTHER* CONSUMER ITEM--

--INSTEAD OF RUSH-ING OFF TO THE NEAREST DOCTOR WITH EVERY LITTLE *TUMOR* OR *HEART ATTACK!*

by TOM TOMORROW

3. WISHFUL THINKING

MOST OF THE UNINSURED ARE ACTUALLY *YOUNG* AND *HEALTHY!*

THEY'RE PROBABLY HAVING FABULOUS SEX IN EXOTIC VACATION LOCALES EVEN AS WE *SPEAK!*

4. FEARMONGERING

UP IN *CANADA*, THEY HAVE *LONG WAITS* AND *ANNOYING BUREAU-CRACIES!*

UNLIKE *OUR* SYSTEM, IN WHICH THESE THINGS ARE *UNHEARD* OF!

7. SELECTIVE CONTEMPT

THE GOVERNMENT WILL RUN HEALTH CARE LIKE IT RAN *KATRINA!*

HA, HA! GOVERNMENT CAN'T DO *ANYTHING* RIGHT!

EXCEPT, UM, THE THINGS *WE* SUPPORT.

8. SHEER CHUTZPAH

WHY ARE WE EVEN DIS-CUSSING THIS? THERE *IS* NO HEALTH CARE CRISIS!

MICHAEL MOORE MADE THE WHOLE THING UP--TO SELL *MOVIE TICKETS!*

MAKES PER-FECT SENSE TO *ME!*

TOM TOMORROW©2007... www.thismodernworld.com

Introduction

Although some of the best health care in the world can be found in the United States, ours is also one of the most inequitable systems in the world. While the well-insured get all the high-tech health care money can buy, nearly 100 million Americans who are underinsured or uninsured are denied access to health care, suffer greatly, and have life expectancy rates that are much lower than those who are well-insured. And it's a system in which just about all of us are vulnerable.

How did this happen in a country where we spent $2.1 trillion in 2006—more than $7,000 per person—on health care, an extraordinary cost that has nearly doubled in the past decade? How did we become the only western nation not to provide comprehensive health care to everyone, despite outspending all other countries nearly two to one? Why are we spending all of our time talking about health *insurance* instead of health *care*? The problem, according to Dr. Arnold Relman, former editor of the *New England Journal of Medicine*, "is the extent to which the insurance and delivery of our medical care is governed by commerce and private enterprise rather than by public regulation and social need."

Our hope is that this book will help decipher the jargon, provide an introduction to the basic facts and arguments about health care, and make the case for a system of national health care—which is quite simply the only way we will be able to make first-rate care available cost-effectively and equitably.

10 Excellent Reasons for National Health Care gives voice to nurses, patients, doctors, health policy experts, scholars, labor leaders, and activists, each of whom brings different perspectives and experiences to their views about health care. Nevertheless, each believes—and eloquently argues—that health care is a basic human right. As with the civil rights movement, social justice did not begin to occur until the public cried out for it. Already Americans favor publicly funded national health care by a two-to-one margin, as do a majority of physicians, two former Surgeons General, and numerous medical organizations. Now we must begin to make our voices heard.

In addition to helping the reader understand all of the arguments—moral, economic, medical, and practical—in favor of single-payer national health care, *10 Excellent Reasons for National Health Care* also aims to dispel the many myths that exist about it. Single-payer national health care is not socialized medicine. It is not a "government takeover" of health care. It will leave the delivery of health care pretty much as it is. However, in a single-payer system, health care funding would be managed by a single public agency that directly pays doctors, hospitals, and other medical providers, eliminating the expensive middleman—private *for-profit* health insurance companies.

People are often surprised to learn that we already have such a system in place for our seniors and the permanently disabled: it's called Medicare. Medicare does an admirably efficient, cost-effective job of paying health care bills; the contributors to this book believe that a single-payer system that expanded Medicare to cover all residents of the United States would be the simplest and most efficacious way to solve our health care crisis. Since Medicare does not currently include everything needed for truly comprehensive health care, those services not currently included would need to be added. One way to think of it is as "improved, expanded Medicare for all," which is also the name of HR 676, the bill that Congressman John Conyers Jr., along with eighty-eight co-sponsors, has introduced.

Having an efficient single-payer mechanism would save so many billions of dollars that *all* Americans would be able to have secure, fair, comprehensive health care. Dr. Irving J. Selikoff, the late doctor who exposed the wrongdoing of the asbestos industry (and after whom the environmental and occupational health division at New York's Mt. Sinai Hospital Center for Occupational and Environmental Medicine was named) once said, "Statistics are human beings with the tears wiped away."

In this book you will see lots of numbers about the millions who are uninsured, underinsured, bankrupt, sick, or dying as a consequence of our broken-down, profit-driven health insurance system. As you read those numbers, we hope you remember Dr. Selikoff's words—and then join us in the crucial effort to make health care a right for everyone.

—Mary E. O'Brien and
Martha Livingston

1

It's good for our health

Martha Livingston

Most of the time, most of us don't need health care. What happens in our daily lives has at least as much impact on our health as whether or not we have health insurance. Do we have a home that's not too cold in winter or too hot in summer, not too crowded, in a clean, safe environment? Do we have enough of the right kinds of foods to eat? Do we have satisfying work that pays enough for us to afford a decent life? Do we have time to enjoy our families and friends? Are our kids and our elders well cared for? Or are we living in a stressful, overcrowded environment, working too many unpleasant hours just to get by, eating on the run? Our health is usually affected much more by these life circumstances than by health care.

But—of course—we all need health care some of the time. Part of being able to live a healthy life is having an ongoing relationship with a health care professional who knows our lives as well as our lab results. Our doctor may

Martha Livingston, PhD, is Associate Professor of Health and Society at the State University of New York College at Old Westbury.

provide suggestions about habits we can change to improve our health, may send us to a nutritionist, may recommend physical activity, may recognize aspects of our home, neighborhood, and working environment that are affecting our health, may prescribe medication, may discover potentially serious conditions before we know they're there, and so forth. This is called primary care, and it's crucial to our well-being. Primary care doctors and nurse-practitioners like to call this relationship our "medical home."

Having such an ongoing relationship becomes absolutely critical, of course, when we're sick. Primary care, far less expensive than critical or emergency care, is what we most often go without when we aren't insured or when we have high-deductible insurance policies or coverage that excludes routine or preventive care. Insurance companies, knowing that they are not likely to be covering the same lives (yes, they call us "covered lives," not people) for very long, cynically save money by not paying for preventive care, even though the system as a whole becomes more expensive, and our health suffers as a result, when we become sicker and turn up for emergency care later on.

With national health insurance, we'd be able to choose any doctor, nurse-practitioner, midwife, or other caregiver. Even those of us who have private insurance now are often quite limited in our choice of caregiver, depending on which caregivers participate in the insurance plan chosen by our employer. Employers, increasingly strapped by escalating health care costs, may change insurance plans year by year, forcing us to change primary-care providers because insurance plans include limited panels of doctors, which makes having a long-term relationship with a caregiver, a "medical home," close to impossible.

For those of us who are uninsured or underinsured, it's even harder to find a medical home. Safety-net providers such as hospital-based health clinics do their best with limited resources, but continuity of care—seeing the same doctor or nurse-practitioner—is a luxury they're not able to offer. Once finished with their medical training, medical interns and residents move on.

Of course, the lack of a medical home is not the only consequence for those tens of millions who are uninsured or underinsured. Often they are simply unable to get help when they need it. The result is tragic: the health of millions of us is a good deal worse than it could be, and many thousands of Americans will prematurely get sick or die. The latest analyses estimate that anywhere from 22,000 to 101,000 Americans die every year of treatable conditions simply because they were uninsured and could not get timely care.[1,2]

But the problem is much, much larger than that. Think about the major, common health problems in the United States: heart disease, cancer, diabetes. There are about 21 million Americans with diabetes—and millions of them don't even know it. Diabetes is a silent condition. Americans without access to routine checkups may not learn that they have this life-threatening condition until many years later, when they turn up in emergency rooms with heart attacks, kidney failure, and other killer diseases. The same can be said for hypertension, which leads to death and disability from heart disease and stroke.

Well-insured Americans with cancer live longer and survive their disease at a much higher rate than under- or uninsured Americans, primarily because they get diagnosed and treated more quickly and by better specialists.[3] American women are dying of an almost completely treatable condition, cervical cancer, because they lack access to a simple Pap smear, considered "routine" and therefore very often not covered.[4]

Many women in the United States can't get prenatal care, although the astronomical cost of treating even one seriously ill newborn could pay for prenatal care for hundreds of women. We do quite badly in terms of infant mortality, worse than twenty-six other countries in the world; close to seven of every thousand U.S. babies die before their first birthday, compared with three or fewer in Iceland, Sweden, Luxembourg, and Japan.[5] Our neonatal mortality (death before twenty-eight days of age) ranks behind all but one of thirty-three countries.[6] Women in the United States are more likely to die in childbirth than women in thirty-two other nations—including all of the other wealthy nations and some a good deal less wealthy than we (e.g., Latvia).[7]

On life expectancy, the ultimate health outcome, Americans fare worse than our counterparts in all of the other wealthy countries: we rank twenty-second for men, who live, on average, to 75.2 years, and twenty-third for women, at 80.4 years.[8]

While access to health care isn't responsible for all health outcomes, it's part of the picture, and that picture, in the United States, is shameful: people get sicker, and die sooner, because they cannot get health care when they need it. These health outcomes aren't limited only to the un- and underinsured; when some of us can't get care, and get sicker, everyone's health suffers. Consider, for example, the woman coughing near you on the subway. Might she have untreated, and contagious, TB? Wouldn't it be reassuring to know that she and all of our neighbors were able to seek medical care when they needed it?

Clearly, we can do better. All of the other wealthy, industrialized countries in the world have; they all have some form of national health care, in which people can get health care when they need it without having to worry about where the money will come from. No one's system is perfect; each nation's health care is paid for, organized, and delivered differently, in accordance with that nation's history and culture.[9] (In fact, in Japan people see the doctor much more frequently, and spend many more days in the hospital, than in any other wealthy nation. And in Germany, spa treatments are considered medically necessary for some patients.)

How countries pay for care also varies: Milton I. Roemer refers to the "continuum of government intervention," ranging from the United States's free-market approach to financing care through a single-payer or similar system (known as national health insurance, such as in Canada), to organizing the delivery of care (known as a national health service, such as in the United Kingdom), to social-ized medicine, in which the government owns the health care facilities and employs the health care workers and professionals (such as the Veterans Administration sys-tem in the United States, or the national system in Cuba).[10] It should be noted that while private insurance plays a role in some European systems, that role is quite small, and it is highly regulated.

How doctors and other health care professionals are paid varies as well. In some countries, doctors are on salary; in some, doctors are paid a fixed amount per patient on their roster (known as a capitation system). In some, doctors and other caregivers are paid for each service they pro-vide; that's called "fee-for-service." There are strengths and drawbacks to each method of payment; for example, in a fee-for-service system, doctors are not adequately re-imbursed for lengthy office visits and patient education, but for *doing things*.

Of course, as patients, we don't think about payment mechanisms; we think about health care. We experience the consequences of different systems but aren't aware of them.

Most countries allow doctors to practice both within the national system and outside it, in private practice. This may make a particular specialist hard to get to see in the public system; time spent seeing private patients is, after all, time not available to national health system patients. One strength of Canada's system is that doctors are not allowed to provide medically necessary care both publicly and privately. As a result, very few Canadian doctors—just over one hundred nationwide, in 2006—choose to "opt out" of the public system.[11] Canadians are especially proud of the equity that this aspect of their system affords to all.

Simply guaranteeing that people have access to needed health care hasn't meant, in Canada or elsewhere, that such debates are settled; far from it. Rather, it creates the possibility of a national discussion about how health care might best be organized and delivered.

We in the United States have been subjected to a drumbeat of mis- and disinformation about national health care systems, because it's an effective way to scare Americans, the majority of whom, according to the polls, are eager for the government to take control over a clearly broken health insurance system.[12] Opponents of a Medicare-for-All solution to our health care mess refer to our plan as "socialized medicine," which it clearly is not. The most common myths are that people in other countries have to wait in line for urgently needed care, that care is rationed, and that those rich enough to do so come to the United States for care unavailable to them in their home countries. These myths get repeated over and over despite there being little evidence in support of these claims. I'm most familiar with myths about Canada's health care system, having lived and studied there.

At age seventy-three, Peter Smollett, a retired film professor living in Toronto who had had mild, stable angina (chest pain) for ten years and hypertension for twenty years as well as Type 2 diabetes, experienced severe, unstable angina. He was admitted to the hospital immediately and found to require quadruple bypass surgery as well as a heart valve replacement. He was referred to the best surgeon in Toronto, was transferred to that surgeon's hospital, and had the surgery within days. His wife, Eleanor, also a retired professor, reported some weeks later, after Peter's successful surgery and discharge with home nursing, "For your health advocacy work, you might be interested in knowing of our out-of-pocket costs to date (26 days in hospital): in-hospital dentistry required before surgery could proceed, about $200; hospital phone connection, about $20; bedside television rental, about

$330; hospital bed rental and delivery, about $200; extra local transport—taxis, subway, parking—about $150; extra phoning, snacks out, etc., about $50. Total: about $950 (then about $750 U.S.[13])." Several years earlier, Peter had been treated for a rare cancer of the neck. Because he resides in Canada, he was able to locate and be treated by the most knowledgeable doctor on his rare condition, and his care was world class in that situation as well.

Throughout the United States, the richest country in the world with the most expensive health care in the world, uninsured people are lining up at free clinics run by medical professionals and students to get care they can't get anywhere else. Larry Towell and Sara Corbett, in a 2007 photo essay, documented a three-day annual health care "fair" in Virginia run by a group that spends most of its year bringing care to Haiti, India, Tanzania, and other poor countries.[14] From Friday morning to Sunday night, doctors, dentists, and nurses work in tents to bring some relief to Americans who are, in a sense, medically homeless. Patients needing treatment, from dental care to cancer care, are seen in this marathon; hundreds are turned away because the demand is just too great. One emergency-room doctor volunteering at the "fair" said, "If you spend a day here, you see there's something wrong with health care in this country." Scenes like this could play out every day in cities and towns across the country, in free clinics.

From France to Japan, from Australia to Norway, in every other industrialized nation in the world, people are able to get the care they need. The United States is alone in failing to provide care to all. It's time for us to join the rest of the wealthy nations of the world and give every one of us, not just some lucky ones, a medical home at last.

2

It costs less and saves money (unlike all of the alternatives)

Leonard Rodberg

Everyone knows that health care in America costs too much. Whether you look at the middle-class Americans who can no longer afford to insure their families or you compare the United States with other countries, you have to conclude that there is something wrong with the way we have set up our health care system.

Coverage for an average family through employer-based private insurance now costs more than $12,000 each year; it is nearly $4,500 for a single individual.[1] Since the median family income in the United States is now $59,894, one-half of all American families would have to spend 20 percent or more of their income to buy health insurance.[2] Clearly millions of middle-class families cannot afford to purchase health insurance today.

If we compare the United States with other countries, we find that in 2006 we were spending more than $7,026[3] for every person in this country, while the typical advanced

Leonard Rodberg, PhD, is Professor and Chair of the Urban Studies Department at Queens College/CUNY.

country elsewhere in the world is spending just $3,840 per person.[4] In fact, the country with the next most expensive health care system, Switzerland, is spending just 70 percent of what we are spending.

How can we make sense of this? Why does the United States stand out as having the most expensive health care in the world? Is it that we provide the best care and are thus the healthiest in the world? Far from it. In fact, on almost every measure—except cost—we are very far from the leader. According to the most recent international data, we are twenty-fifth in life expectancy among the world's advanced countries, twenty-seventh in infant mortality, and fifteenth in deaths before age seventy-five that are potentially preventable with timely and appropriate medical care.[5] And Americans are not satisfied with their system: we're fourteenth in the world in the public's satisfaction with their health care system.[6]

Then why are we spending so much? The answer is actually quite straightforward, if we compare how we pay for health care with the financing method of every other country. The United States is the exception, the outlier: *we are the only country that uses private, for-profit insurance to finance health care for the majority of its population.*[7] Every other country uses either a public fund to pay for health care or private nonprofit funds that are heavily regulated by government. Insurers in other countries cannot spend money avoiding sick people, as our for-profit insurers do, through "underwriting," nor can they devise ways to shift their expenses onto the government. Furthermore, every one of these countries uses its funds to cover everyone, not just those who can afford to pay or whose employers can afford to pay, as in this country.

The question for the United States is: Can we reduce the cost of health care and, at the same time, see that everyone has access to the care they need, without cutting back on either the amount of care or its quality? The short answer is that we can. And we can do this not by reducing our access to doctors and hospitals or to valuable new technology—the MRIs, the CAT scans, and the intensive care facilities—or on the lifesaving medications developed over the past few decades, but by eliminating the wasteful administrative and billing costs that gobble up increasing portions of our health care dollar.

At the same time, while we want to reduce waste, we also want to hold down costs in the future. It turns out that the same approach that will reduce waste and inefficiency will also provide us with mechanisms for containing costs going forward. We can cut administrative waste and make better use of the resources we have by planning our investments better, avoiding duplicate purchases, and using our facilities more wisely.

We can get a clue as to how we can reduce costs by looking at what it would cost to provide health care to those who are currently uninsured. The cost of providing full care to the uninsured—who today receive only one-half as much care as those who have good insurance—has been estimated by the Urban Institute to be between $40 billion and $60 billion annually.[8] But any proposal that would end up covering the uninsured through *private* insurance—for instance, through a so-called "individual mandate" that would require everyone who doesn't receive insurance from their employer to purchase it—would add upward of $150 billion in additional spending by individuals, government, or both.[9]

Comparing ourselves with other countries, then, suggests that our current reliance on private insurance adds enormous cost to the system without actually increasing the amount of care delivered or improving the quality of that care. We can see this in part directly from the insurance companies' own balance sheets. They show that what they spend on medical care (they call this their "medical loss ratio") is about 80 percent of their total revenue.[10] That is, the cost of processing claims, marketing (advertising and payments to their salespeople), "underwriting" (determining whether they are actually willing to insure an individual or group, and at what price), "utilization reviews" (checking on whether to approve the care that doctors want to provide and medications they want to prescribe), and profits consume 20 cents out of every dollar. All of this expense adds nothing to patient care.

By contrast, the federally run Medicare program, which

pays for health care for more than 40 million seniors and persons with disabilities, spends 97 cents of every dollar on patient care.[11] So one way to think of our health care system is that the insurance companies are wasting 17 cents out of every dollar. Nothing of any value to our health is gained by the insurance companies' spending that money on their own administration and profit.

But that's not all. The presence of dozens of insurance companies in any community, each offering hundreds of different plans, means that every provider of health care— every doctor, every hospital, every lab, every imaging facility—has to hire people to deal with these insurance companies: to call them for approval of treatment, to contact them to find out if patients are covered for particular treatments or procedures, and then to bill patients for the costs that insurance won't cover. All of us have dealt with these people whenever we have gone to a doctor or hospital for medical care. In fact, the first person you usually see when you enter a doctor's office or a hospital admitting office is the billing clerk!

It's estimated that all of these billing-related costs add at least 10 percent to the cost of health care.[12] None of this would be needed in a system where there was comprehensive coverage for everyone and one fund that provided that coverage.

There are other costs as well to our current system, costs that often go uncounted but that are just as real.

A county legislator in New York has spoken of the myriad hidden ways in which our fragmented health system costs his county money: the staff that helps frail seniors navigate the complexities of the health care and reimbursement systems, the benefits managers negotiating with insurance companies and then assisting employees in dealing with their health insurance claims, the loss of productive work time when employees consult with the benefits manager and fight insurance company denials, the staff time devoted to collective bargaining on health care issues, the staff time devoted to developing and publicizing a discount prescription card for county residents without insurance, the staff time devoted to collecting fees from private insurers for the health services these agencies provide, the people waiting in jail until payment for drug or alcohol treatment can be assured, and the staff in local agencies working on getting these inmates into health care programs that will cover their treatment.[13]

There are, as well, the young businesses in the county that do not get started because they cannot offer a health plan and can't attract the employees they need, the employees who don't like their jobs and perform at less than the desired level but remain because they need the health insurance, and the nurses and other health care professionals who routinely leave direct patient care positions to take jobs with insurance companies, contributing to the severe shortage of nurses and physicians. None of these costs are included in cost comparisons between single payer and our present system, but, as this county leader said, "Every one of them would go away if there was a single, simple and consistent answer to the question, 'Who will pay?'"

Thus, moving to a single comprehensive plan provided through a single payer—a program like the existing federal Medicare program that efficiently covers the elderly and the disabled—would save 30 percent of the cost of the care now financed through private insurance and at least 10 percent of the care funded through public systems, as well as all of these ancillary costs that are never counted. More than half of all medical care is already paid for with public funds through Medicare, Medicaid, and other public health programs. Putting these together, the overall system savings from moving to a single-payer system would then amount to about 15 percent of total current expenditures, or $350 billion each year at current costs. *In fact, numerous studies conducted since the early 1990s show that these savings would be sufficient to fund comprehensive health care for all those who are currently uninsured and underinsured.*[14]

Shifting to a single-payer system would not only provide significant cost savings but also permit us to slow the seemingly inexorable increase every year in the cost of health care. For forty years now, the annual cost of health care has been rising at a minimum of twice the rate of general inflation. Just between 2000 and 2006, the cost of health care rose 87 percent, compared to a general inflation rate in the same period of 18 percent.[15]

There are many reasons for these cost increases: the introduction of new technology, the rising cost of pharmaceuticals, increased specialization in the medical profession, and other factors. However, again, a comparison with other countries shows that although they have introduced and are using exactly the same technology, they have been far more successful in containing the cost of health care.[16] How is this possible?

The answer is the same as for the high costs themselves: there is no way, in a system that uses many independent private insurance companies, to contain these rising costs. Only when a single entity funds and oversees new investments is it possible to invest wisely and carefully in these new technologies. The Veterans Administration, for instance, widely recognized as one of the best health care systems in the country, shows how successfully and efficiently health care can be delivered when it is planned with the needs of the patient in mind.[17]

Having a method of planning and budgeting does not mean denying ourselves access to these potentially lifesaving techniques; it means implementing them in an intelligent way that makes the best use of both the technologies and our dollars. Systems like the Veterans Administration have shown that it is possible to provide excellent medical care while making very efficient use of the dollars given them.[18]

Any plan that claims to achieve universal health care by relying on private insurance will inevitably add more than $100 billion to what we are already spending for health care. By contrast, moving to a simple, single-payer Medicare-for-All program would allow everyone to be covered without spending any more than we are spending now, and it would give us the tools that would allow us at last, to get control over the ever-rising cost of health care.

How would it be paid for? There are many different ways that the money might be raised, but the guiding principle should be that the financing mechanism is equitable and fair. Employers should contribute, since many are already paying for health insurance for their employees, but individuals and families should contribute as well, according to their means. Rep. John Conyers Jr. (D-MI), principal sponsor of HR 676, the United States National Health Insurance Act, or "Expanded and Improved Medicare for All," would fund it through a combination of a 3.3 percent payroll tax on employers and employees, a stock transfer tax, and an income tax surcharge on the richest 5 percent of taxpayers and by reversing the 2001 and 2002 tax cuts on the wealthy.[19] Another approach would fund it solely through a payroll tax, 8.17 percent on employers and 3.78 percent on employees making more than $7,000 per year.[20] Regardless of the method used, the nation, along with most of its people and employers, would be paying less for health care under such a publicly funded single-payer plan than it is now. We can have better health care that costs less.

3

It will assure high-quality health care for all Americans, rich or poor

Mary E. O'Brien

Every summer I volunteer in the Tutwiler Clinic in the Mississippi Delta, one of the poorest areas in the country. For the Catholic nuns who operate the clinic, treatment never depends on payment; the nuns make ends meet through Medicare, Medicaid, the occasional insurance reimbursement, and charity. The quality of care is extraordinarily high by any standard, yet here the inequities of our health care system are dramatic. The starkest example of these inequities is the fact that many of my patients at the clinic simply have no expectation of being healthy as adults. They are poor and historically have not had access to qualified, caring doctors.

One Monday morning I arrived at the clinic to find a muscular, middle-aged man waiting outside the clinic door, holding his ear and in obvious pain. He said he just

Mary E. O'Brien, MD, is a primary care internist at Columbia University Health Services and a faculty member at the Columbia College of Physicians and Surgeons.

wanted ear drops because he had to get to work or he'd lose a day's pay. When I examined his ear it was apparent he had a severe infection in his ear canal and outer ear. It is a condition rarely seen in healthy people, but it is a clear sign of uncontrolled diabetes. His blood sugar was five times normal, and it would have to be controlled before his ear infection would even respond to antibiotics. His blood pressure was sky high and he had a fever.

I explained all of this to him and urged him to go to the hospital in Clarksdale for immediate hospitalization. He looked at me as if I had two heads. "Sorry, Ma'am, but I just want drops for the ear and I'll go back to work. My boss is going to be angry because I'm late right now." Over the past few months he had lost about ten pounds and was constantly thirsty, two common signs of diabetes. He had attributed his weight loss and thirstiness to hard farm work in the hot Mississippi sun. He hadn't seen a doctor in years and had no idea that he had dangerously high blood pressure and diabetes. Although he had worked on the same plantation for twenty years and was now a foreman, he had neither health insurance nor an allowance for sick time. As to my suggestion of going to the hospital in Clarksdale, he flatly refused to consider it.

Over the next few hours at the clinic we gave him intravenous fluids and insulin to start bringing down his blood sugar, and we started intravenous (IV) antibiotics for the ear infection and blood pressure medications. He agreed to come back twice a day, before and after work, to get insulin and IV antibiotics and to learn how to treat his diabetes and high blood pressure. By the end of the week he looked much better. The clinic had provided all of his medicines and his treatment free. I'm sure that if his unbearably painful ear had not forced him to come to the clinic he would have collapsed working in the fields, another casualty of our inadequate health care system. It is estimated that at least 22,000 (and possibly more than 100,000) people die in the United States each year because they do not have health insurance and access to care.[1, 2]

This small clinic can serve only a tiny fraction of the residents of the Delta, most of whom are in desperate need of medical attention. But it offers a vision of the high-quality medical care that could be delivered to all residents of the United States if a single-payer health program were adopted, one that guarantees access to highly skilled clinicians without charge.

What are the essential elements that are necessary for high-quality health care, and how would a national health care system achieve this?

Access

Quality of health care has little meaning if millions are unable to access care in the first place. We all need to be able to see a doctor when we are sick, so guaranteed and automatic health care coverage from birth to death is a must. This coverage must include not only care for illnesses and injuries but also preventive care, mental health care, medications, dental care, and long-term care.

This concept of access to health care is so important that this year the American Cancer Society has decided to commit its entire $15 million advertising budget to promoting universal health care. Its chief executive, John R. Seffrin, has said, "I believe, if we don't fix the health care system, that lack of access will be a bigger cancer killer than tobacco. The ultimate control of cancer is as much a public policy issue as it is a medical and scientific issue."[3]

Those diagnosed with colon cancer who are uninsured have a 70 percent greater chance of dying within three years. Uninsured women diagnosed with breast cancer suffer an almost 50 percent higher risk of premature death. Halfway measures such as free screening for cancer offer little comfort to the uninsured or underinsured who realize that they will not be able to afford the high cost of treatment.

A Single Standard of Excellent Care

Whom would you point to who does not deserve equal high-quality care? The only way to create an equal opportunity to get high-quality health care is to have a single, comprehensive health care plan for all. This means no bare bones plans whose high deductibles and co-pays effectively exclude us from health care. If the health care system treats all of us equally, then the most powerful among us will make sure that this is a top-notch system.

Our current system compromises the health care of all of us, insured and uninsured alike. Take the example of the severe overcrowding in hospital emergency rooms. Half of U.S. emergency rooms report daily overcrowding, with that number climbing to two-thirds of urban emergency rooms. This can result in vital delays in treatment, while overworked staff struggle to handle all of the patients. Over half a million ambulances are diverted from crowded emergency rooms each year in the United States, delaying lifesaving care for the critically ill. In many areas of the country, specially staffed and equipped trauma centers have closed because they are not profitable, forcing patients to lose those initial critical minutes of care that are so often vital in saving lives. Three-quarters of hospitals have difficulty finding specialists to take emergency or trauma calls. And despite all the rhetoric about preparedness, our overcrowded and underfunded emergency care system is ill prepared to respond to a major disaster—be it a natural one, a disease outbreak, or a terrorist attack.[4]

Choice

We need to have free choice of doctors and hospitals and not be restricted by a managed care plan or a constantly changing list of in-network providers or be excluded entirely if we are uninsured. It is ironic that opponents of national health care cite their fears that Americans would lose freedom of choice under a national plan. Exactly the opposite would be true. With universal access and comprehensive coverage, free choice would be guaranteed. Closely related to this is the need for continuity of care, or what is sometimes referred to as a medical home, where a team of health care professionals including doctors, nurse-practitioners, and nurses knows us and our medical problems, takes care of us appropriately and efficiently, and advocates for the best medical care without any financial conflict of interest. Our care could also be coordinated when we see specialists or are hospitalized, and the number of medical errors caused by poor communication would be reduced.

Quality of Care and Evidence-Based Medicine

The quality of health care and the outcome of different treatments must be measured and monitored so we can constantly fine-tune and improve health care. But that is impossible in our current private system. The for-profit health insurance companies don't study the health or health outcomes of their clients in order to improve their services. Far from it. They monitor those who are sick and expensive to care for and try to exclude or drop them from their plans. In fact, it may surprise you to learn that almost all of the population data we have on the effectiveness of different medical treatments and outcomes come from our government-sponsored public health care programs—Medicare, Medicaid, and the Veterans Administration system.

Under a unified single-payer health care system there would be far greater accountability because we would have medical treatment and health outcomes data for everyone and we could better study and determine effective medical practice. We could monitor physician competency on a nationwide basis and identify the outliers providing poor care.

We rely on the competency of our doctors, but our current fragmented system renders it impossible to track a doctor's performance at an accepted medical standard. A good electronic medical record system could improve a doctor's practice through reminders for recommended screening (like Pap smears, mammograms, and cholesterol checks), guidelines for chronic disease management, and alerts for drug interactions or improper doses of drugs. It could also detect practitioners who are far off the mark for appropriate medical care, something our current system has failed at miserably.

Electronic Medical Records

There is no doubt in anyone's mind—big business, the medical establishment, or the highest levels of government—that a unified secure electronic medical records system must be created. Indeed, every major Democratic presidential candidate has made an electronic medical records system a cornerstone of his or her health care reform package. However, the overarching question is whether a unified electronic medical records program can be realized without a single-payer health care delivery system. Already Microsoft, Google, and Texas Instruments have launched or are about to launch competing electronic medical records systems. It is obvious and predictable that a multiplicity of electronic medical records delivery systems will evolve and the important characteristics of the Veterans Administration's medical records system—unified, affordable, and readily available—will disappear.

What we need is a unified national electronic medical records and information system, one that scrupulously guards our medical privacy and confidentiality while affording health care professionals immediate access to a patient's medical history. Consider the case of a veteran who receives regular treatment at a veterans hospital in New York. If the veteran were to suffer a heart attack or a life-threatening emergency while visiting relatives in southern California, that vet could enter the nearest veterans hospital and the medical staff of that hospital could have access to this vet's entire medical history within seconds, and the staff could then proceed to the most informed course of treatment. The veterans hospital system has in place a unified electronic medical records system that links all of its hospitals. This was invaluable after Hurricane Katrina, when thousands of veterans from New Orleans and surrounding areas sought health care at Veterans Administration facilities throughout the country. Nothing comparable would be possible in our present diffuse and fragmented health care system.

From a public health standpoint, such a unified computerized database would permit early detection of epidemics like a severe flu season and allow prompt immunization to better control it. It would allow careful tracking of the incidence of cancer, heart disease, and depression so we could better study these chronic illnesses and allocate resources appropriately.

We need to combine the information from an electronic national database with strategic thinking to improve our systems for delivering health care to make our health care more efficient and cost effective while always having quality as our primary goal.

Health Planning

Among the many benefits that would flow naturally from eliminating for-profit health insurance companies and financial conflicts of interest would be a clear assessment and allocation of resources—to eliminate expensive redundancy of hospital and radiology facilities and to regionalize specialty surgery in accord with the knowledge that hospitals with a high volume of surgery have better proficiency and patient outcomes than hospitals with low volume. More focus could also be given to preventive health care.

Patient-Physician Relationship

At the heart of excellent health care is a patient's trusting and ongoing relationship with a personal primary care physician. A recent international study by the Commonwealth Fund showed that having a "medical home" where you have a regular doctor who knows your medical history and is easy to reach by phone during business hours and will coordinate your care with other physicians or hospitals is associated with more comprehensive and cost-effective care as well as greater patient satisfaction.

Clinicians need to have the time to listen carefully and respectfully to a patient's problems to determine appropriate, cost-effective treatment. The pressure on doctors to see patients in ten- to fifteen-minute appointments ultimately saves neither time nor money and leads to increasing frustration and medical errors.

A number of years ago I saw an elderly woman in a neighborhood clinic who had no regular doctor but had seen several different doctors over the past year, each of whom had added new and more potent medicines in order to control her blood pressure. She had lots of side effects from these medications, but her blood pressure remained dangerously high. She assured me that she took all of her medicines religiously and she denied adding any salt to her food. I asked her to describe in detail her actual meals: for breakfast, bacon and eggs; for lunch, canned soup; and for dinner, canned beans and rice. It turned out that she was getting a huge amount of salt in her diet that overwhelmed her medicines. She agreed to try to eliminate canned foods, and over several weeks her blood pressure was easily controlled with only two medications. By my taking some extra time to explore her diet and then to educate her to the danger of ingesting large volumes of salt through prepared foods and to explain how her medicines operated in lowering her blood pressure, she was able to understand her high blood pressure and to take an active role in controlling it. If physicians are compelled to treat their patients at an assembly-line rate, too many subtle or complicated diseases will go unnoticed. Only a system dedicated to the optimal care of the patient—versus the optimum profits of insurance companies—will afford doctors the time that is needed to explore and diagnose thoroughly and competently. A single-payer system is the moral and economic answer to our current health care crisis.

The United States stands almost alone in the world in its failure to recognize health care as a human right. Instead we consider health care as an economic commodity. If you can afford it, you can get it. If not, you're out of luck.

—Robert H LeBow, MD, author of *Health Care Meltdown*

4

It's the best choice — morally and economically

Marie Gottschalk

A well-known political scientist once said that the definition of the alternatives is the supreme instrument of power. The simple question — to move to a single-payer health care system or not — conceals major differences over whether to frame the health care issue as primarily an economic question or a moral one. Certainly economic considerations are critical to propelling the cause of universal health care. But economic competitiveness is not the central economic issue at stake in the debate over health care reform.

If we are to finally achieve a fair, affordable, and truly universal health care system, other economic considerations need to be part of the debate. These include: How efficient is the U.S. health system? How is the health care cost burden distributed among business, government, and the public? What are the trends in health care cost shifting? What is (and what should be) the role of insur-

Marie Gottschalk, PhD, is a professor of political science at the University of Pennsylvania.

ance companies in the U.S. health system and the wider political economy? Although it's easy to emphasize the economic rationale for health care reform at the cost of the moral rationale, the two cannot be disentangled. All of these economic issues in some way touch on how to re-divide the economic pie—and that raises basic questions about economic and social justice.

Organized labor has enormous potential to be the pivotal player in raising these economic and moral questions and anchoring a reform coalition that fundamentally reshapes the health care debate. For well over a century now, labor has been instrumental in the development of the U.S. health system. It established some of the first prepaid group practices and health maintenance organizations, was the leading voice for national health insurance up until the mid-1970s, and was decisive in the establishment of Medicare and in the expansion of other major social programs, like Social Security and the Great Society. The employment-based system of health benefits is largely the product of a collective-bargaining regime established during and immediately after World War II. That system is under siege today. Without unions to act as a brake, today's downward spiral in health benefits for union and nonunion workers would be even faster.

Divided and hemorrhaging members, organized labor still has formidable resources to influence the course of health care reform. The membership rolls and resources of the major unions dwarf those of most public interest groups. Labor's lobbying capacity has expanded dramatically as the American Federation of Labor–Congress of Industrial Organizations (AFL-CIO), other labor groups, and individual unions have invested more heavily in lobbyists, enlarged their research departments, and developed grassroots lobbying networks. Labor's financial resources have not contracted significantly despite its dwindling membership base. Today the Democratic Party is more dependent than ever on labor's money, votes, and electoral apparatus. Although money and members are important, they are not decisive in determining the political influence of organized labor. As Douglas A. Fraser, the late former president of the United Automobile Workers, once said, the strength of the union movement also depends "on the agenda, the sense of commitment and the manner in which the labor movement allocates resources."[1]

As we stand at the brink of another major attempt to overhaul the U.S. health care system, organized labor is divided about how to define the alternatives. At one pole is Andrew Stern, president of the Service Employees International Union (SEIU), the nation's largest union, and arguably the best-known labor leader today. He contends that to achieve universal care, health care reform must be pitched primarily as an economic competitiveness issue, not a moral one.[2] Stern also has indicated that the single-payer approach, for all its virtues, is a political nonstarter.

At the other pole are the growing number of national unions, locals, labor councils, and rank-and-file members pledged to the single-payer solution. Somewhere in between is the nation's largest labor federation, which in March 2007 endorsed the idea of Medicare-for-All but carefully avoided mentioning the "s" word—that is, single payer.[3]

So far, Stern has garnered a disproportionate amount of media and popular attention. His business-friendly stance on health care reform, which stresses how the U.S. health care system is fundamentally hurting the country's economic competitiveness, helps explain why. But his economic competitiveness argument is not convincing and could undermine efforts to forge a successful coalition or movement on behalf of affordable, high-quality care for all.

Universal Health Care and Economic Competitiveness

When he broke away from the AFL-CIO in 2005 to form the Change to Win federation, which represents about 6 million workers, Stern implored organized labor to reposition itself on organizing new members and other issues. Yet his position on health care reform is remarkably similar to the pro-business stance that John Sweeney, currently president of the 9-million-member AFL-CIO, maneuvered the federation into as chairman of its health care committee in the lead-up to the battle over the Clinton plan in the early 1990s.[4] Like Sweeney years ago, Stern has focused on courting the business sector. In his view, no fundamental change in health care will "arrive until American business leaders make the call for change."[5]

Stern has long linked the interests of the SEIU with the interests of the business sector. In July 2006, he sent a letter to every Fortune 500 CEO asking them to make health care their national priority. After reading an op-ed on health care reform written by Stern in the *Wall Street Journal,* Safeway chief executive Steve Burd said: "I could have written that."[6] In January 2007, Stern's union launched a new health care coalition with two organizations that have checkered pasts on universal health care—the Business Roundtable, the elite business organization of top CEOs that helped torpedo the Clinton plan, and AARP, the country's largest organization for senior citizens, which gave critical support to the controversial Medicare prescription drug bill in 2003.

Stern's most controversial public alliance is with H. Lee Scott Jr., chief executive officer of Wal-Mart. In February 2007, Stern joined Scott and other business executives to announce the creation of "Better Health Care Together," a business-labor coalition. Despite Wal-Mart's dismal record on health benefits and other labor issues, Stern appears confident that the bottom line provides compelling reasons for Wal-Mart and other large employers to be constructive allies in health reform. "Obviously, we have a huge problem for American business because it is pretty hard to compete in a global economy when the price of your health care is put on the cost of goods, while in other countries, it is shared among society," he contends.[7]

In tapping big business as a key ally in the health care debate beginning in the 1980s, much of organized labor took a stance that was remarkably similar to Stern's position today. Labor leaders largely accepted the Fortune 500's definition of what was ailing the American economy and hence the American worker. Many of them jumped on the competitiveness bandwagon. In their public statements, labor and business leaders regularly shared a simple refrain: higher medical costs were making American products less competitive in the international marketplace, which was in turn severely hurting the U.S. economy and the American worker.

Health care economists have raised numerous objections to the claim that escalating health care costs imperil the economic competitiveness of the United States and the overall health of the U.S. economy. Their analyses, however, have had little impact on what Princeton professor Uwe Reinhardt calls the "shared folklore" that higher health care costs are pricing U.S. products out of the market.[8]

It is true that employer spending on health care, measured as a percentage of after-tax profits, did jump in the late 1990s. But the rise in health care costs as a percentage of profits was due partly to a drop overall in corporate profits as the dot-com and high-technology sectors went bust in the late 1990s. Spending on health care measured as a percentage of after-tax corporate profits declined steadily from 1986 to 2004, except during the 1998–2001 period. More significantly, employer spending on wages and salaries and on total compensation as a percentage of after-tax profits has dropped precipitously since 1986, except during the 1998–2001 period.[9] With health care costs continuing to escalate, employers have had great success at squeezing wages and other forms of compensation and shifting more health care costs onto their employees. Wages and salaries constitute the smallest portion of the country's gross domestic product (GDP) since the government began collecting such data in 1947. In 2006, on the eve of the subprime crisis and the recession, corporate profits were at their highest level in four decades. This prompted U.S. Bancorp, the investment bank, to declare that we are living in "the golden era of profitability."[10]

To underscore the exceptional severity of the health care cost crunch, Stern and some business leaders stress what U.S. employers are paying out in direct costs for health care as compared to what their foreign competitors pay. They regularly single out the crippling medical expenses that add $1,500 to the cost of each car manufactured by General Motors and note that some of its competitors pay as little as $200 per vehicle.[11] The focus on comparing what U.S. companies pay *directly* for health care relative to what their foreign competitors pay directly skews the health care debate. It ignores the higher indirect costs that many European and Japanese firms and individuals shoulder because of higher corporate and personal income taxes to support more extensive public welfare states. In fact, this amount generally exceeds what even the most generous U.S. firms spend on health care for their employees. "The cost of employment-related health benefits as a percentage of payroll is nearly 50 percent greater in Germany than in the United States, but little is heard about this," according to health care economist Mark Pauly.[12] Many European and Japanese firms are thus highly competitive even though their workers enjoy more generous health, vacation, maternity, and other benefits.

In the early 1990s, the failed Clinton plan, which caused such an uproar with much of the business sector, called for larger employers to contribute a modest 7.9 percent of their payroll to help pay for employees' health coverage. According to Drew Altman, president of the Henry J. Kaiser Family Foundation, "You couldn't have done more to pay off corporate America than they did with the Clinton plan, but in the end, companies turned on it because it was viewed as a big government plan."[13] Since labor leaders' claims that employers were ready to do the right thing on health care (until they weren't) were so persuasive, when business walked away from the table, there was no sustained grassroots pressure to bring it back.

The persistent faith that business will somehow unlock the door to universal, affordable health care flies in the face of the experience of other countries. Although analysts may disagree about precisely why universal and near-universal health care took root in western Europe and Canada, they concur that business was at best a passive player and at worst a hostile force. Studies of the politics of health policy in other countries reveal that the medical providers, the business sector, and other conservative political forces often fiercely opposed the establishment of universal health care.

The Bottom Line

As we gear up for another major debate over universal health care, what economic factors should be stressed? First, the focus needs to stay squarely on the question of who bears the greatest burden of rising health care costs. There is a health care crisis in the United States, but it is a health care crisis with wrenching economic consequences for individuals and households, not employers. Emphasizing what U.S. employers pay out directly for health insurance obscures who really foots the U.S. health care bill. Government expenditures account for about 36 percent of the tab. Household spending comes in next at 33 percent, and employers are in third place at 27 percent.[14] The burden on households is even greater than these figures suggest because "individuals ultimately bear the responsibility of paying for health care through taxes, reduced earnings, and higher product costs."[15]

The economic competitiveness framework obscures the fact that employers and insurers have been remarkably successful at shifting health care costs onto employees, their families, and other individuals through higher co-pays, higher deductibles, restrictions on coverage, and other measures.[16] Since the demise of the Clinton health plan, the benefits of unionized workers have come under attack from many directions. The erosion of benefits in unionized jobs has hastened the erosion of benefits for workers in nonunion jobs. Some employers are eliminating benefits altogether; others are whittling away at them. Companies are creatively using bankruptcy proceedings to wiggle out of contract obligations to unionized workers, in some cases even suing their retirees in an effort to renege on earlier promises made. New national accounting standards for private and public employers threaten to hollow out retiree benefits further. In the public sector, the new standards pit taxpayers against state and municipal employees. Even the U.S. government has been complicit in this assault on employee benefits, with the U.S. Labor Department refusing to take up the cause of retired workers denied promised health benefits, arguing that they "aren't our constituents anymore."[17]

Another important economic question has to do with economic efficiency. The United States has the most expensive, inefficient health care system in the world, with great variations in quality. The country spends over 15 percent of its GDP on health care, yet has 47 million people who are uninsured and millions more who are underinsured. By comparison, other industrialized countries have been able to achieve universal care while spending on average about 9 percent of their GDP on health care.[18] The United States spends much more, yet has fewer hospital beds, doctors, and nurses per capita than many other industrialized countries.[19] No wonder that only 40 percent of Americans describe themselves as satisfied with the U.S. medical system, making the United States nearly last in public satisfaction (and dead last among public health experts polled).[20]

One reason the U.S. health care system is so expensive is that it is so highly regulated by the private insurance industry. The main difference between here and other countries is that the commercial insurers—not the government—are the prime regulators. They determine, with little public input, who is fit to be insured and who is not; which medical bills to pay and which to deny; and which treatments are "experimental" and which are not. These regulations are expensive and have created what Henry Aaron characterizes as "an administrative monstrosity."[21] In 2006, Wellpoint, the country's largest for-profit insurer, spent nearly $9 billion in marketing and administrative costs, many of which involved "regulating" the insurance market.[22] Despite these high marketing and administrative costs, the health insurers are incredibly profitable. In 2006, the six largest health insurance companies had combined profits of more than $10 billion.[23] Ironically, the costs of administering the U.S. health system roughly equal what employers pay out directly for health care—or about one-quarter of total spending on health care in the United States.[24] These calculations for administrative costs do not include all the time wasted as patients chase down referrals, wade through piles of incomprehensible medical bills, and navigate phone trees that take them nowhere. Streamlining U.S. administrative costs to levels comparable to Canada would reduce the U.S. health tab by an estimated 17 percent.[25]

Another important economic question is: Who or what is to blame for health care inflation? The recent stampede to enact health care legislation based on an individual mandate that penalizes people without insurance reinforces the mistaken notion that the uninsured are the prime culprits. Fingers are pointed at the sickly uninsured who rely on expensive emergency room care and at the young and healthy who forgo insurance because they cannot imagine falling ill and needing expensive medical care. As one analyst remarked, attempting to solve the problem of the uninsured by mandating they buy insurance is akin to attempting to solve world hunger by ordering the hungry to buy food. The real culprit is the *expansive* for-profit health care system with its high administrative and marketing costs; the perverse incentives to perform high-cost medical procedures and not invest in primary care, preventive care, and public health; and the enormous economic and there-fore political clout of the pharmaceutical companies and other health care industries.

The bottom line is that to achieve universal health care, the country needs to have real cost containment and to fundamentally reallocate its health care resources. If we are truly committed to creating a high-quality, affordable, universal health care system, someone will have to give something up, and some will have to give up more than others. The call for health care reform in the name of eco-nomic competitiveness holds out the chimera that a win-win solution is possible for all the stakeholders in the health care system—insurers, medical providers, and the general population.

A Dose of Political Realism

The economic rationales for national health insurance are considerable. But we need to resist the temptation to re-duce this mainly to a question of dollars and cents. As Pro-fessor Uwe Reinhardt recently said on *Oprah*, the health care debate really boils down to one question: "Should the child of a gas station attendant have the same chance of staying healthy or getting cured, if sick, as the child of a corporate executive?" Reinhardt went on to note that it would cost about $100 billion in additional government spending to get health care for every man, woman, and child in the United States—or about what the country spends every nine months to fund the war in Iraq.

Successful reform movements in the United States— the abolitionist movement, the New Deal, the civil rights movement—have always had strong moral overtones. President Franklin D. Roosevelt did not invoke the dollars-and-cents language of an accountant to spur the country to support the landmark social insurance programs that became known as the second New Deal.

The New Deal example is relevant in another respect. In the 1930s, the popular Townsend movement of older Americans took the country by storm. This movement in-duced FDR and business to support Social Security and other social welfare protections so as to neutralize grow-ing public sentiment for more radical pension proposals. Facing not only ruinous economic competition at the time but also a burgeoning and threatening social movement, employers decided to accept some legislated solution. As labor economist John Commons once said, employers never accept social responsibility "until they are faced by an alternative which seems worse to them than the one they 'willingly' accept."[26]

It is reasonable to raise the question whether the pursuit of a single-payer strategy is realistic given how politically and economically entrenched the drug and insurance industries are and how entrenched the for-profit medical system is. But Stern and others are wrong to claim that single-payer is a dead end because Americans deeply mistrust the government, are basically satisfied with their health care system, and don't like anyone else's system.[27] This view is not supported by recent public opinion data showing strong public support for a government guarantee of health care.[28] Moreover, a revealing new study of voter discontent by the Democracy Corps found the most commonly chosen phrase to characterize what's wrong with the country was "Big business gets whatever they want in Washington."[29] Perhaps the time has come to ride what *New York Times* columnist Paul Krugman has characterized as the "strong populist tide running in America right now." As the famous German sociologist Max Weber once said: "Successful politics is always the art of the possible. It is no less true, however, that the possible is often achieved only by reaching out towards the impossible which lies beyond it."

You might think you don't have to worry about paying for medical care if you have health insurance. But you would be wrong.

—*Consumer Reports*, "Are You Really
   Covered?"

5

It may be a matter of life or death

Nathan Wilkes

Before the Flood

For years, I never gave my health insurance much thought. As a child and then a student, I always had coverage through my parents' plan. When I was graduated from college and began working for a large telecommunications company, I soon had my own plan as part of the employment benefits package. I understood that if I needed medical care I would get whatever was allowed by my plan, which seemed like a lot. I never paid attention to the cost of the premiums, because my employer paid for most of it before my payroll deduction. When it was time for my annual checkup, I picked a doctor from the in-network list of doctors, paid a co-pay, and that was it.

That's how things were for many years. Every year, the plan would change. Sometimes it was a new insurance company with a new provider network; sometimes we paid a little more for co-pays and prescriptions. I didn't think about it because I didn't really have to.

Nathan Wilkes is an entrepreneur and devoted father who lectures on patient advocacy and emergency preparedness.

A few companies and several years later, my wife and I decided to start a family. My employer always made sure that we had excellent benefits, utilizing a preferred provider organization (PPO) plan. As long as we stayed in-network, out-of-pocket expenses would be minimal. Our first child was born in 2001 at an in-network hospital by an in-network doctor and our total out-of-pocket expense was $500. Going into it, we had thought it was only going to be $250, but the insurance company counted my wife and my newborn daughter as two separate patients, each with a $250 hospital inpatient co-pay.

Two years later, working for the same company and with a similar PPO plan, we had our second child. A little older and a little wiser, I made sure to ask specifically about whether or not we would be hit with two co-pays. We made sure that our OB/GYN was still in-network, and we made plans to deliver at the best in-network hospital in the area.

Our Happy Day

Thomas was born August 6, 2003, and we were proud parents once again. Less than twenty-four hours later our world was turned upside down. This would be the first of many life-changing events to come.

Thomas was circumcised, but his bleeding didn't stop. Our pediatrician had stopped by to check on him and told the hospital to run some blood tests. Later that day, he became very emotional as he broke the news that Thomas had severe hemophilia A, a genetic disorder that prevents his blood from clotting when necessary. He put us in touch with the local Hemophilia Treatment Center, and within a few hours the chief hematologist was in our room explaining how we were going to treat it and reassuring us that it was a manageable disease. She would administer a single dose of anti-hemophilic clotting factor to replace the clotting factor his body would never make on its own. This would control his current bleed, and we would keep an eye on it to make sure that was sufficient. We knew that he would need to receive clotting factor for the rest of his life, but we didn't know how expensive it would be.

The hospital moved Thomas into the Neonatal Intensive Care Unit (NICU) so the hematologist (who was not part of the hospital or NICU staff) could start an IV in our little guy, give the factor, and make him better.

He was in the NICU for a little more than a day. We never left his side. It was odd seeing our little one in the NICU, because he was nearly ten pounds in a room full of preemies less than half his size in oxygen chambers. In fact, the NICU nurses did little more than check his vitals a few times while we were there. They had never even seen anti-hemophilic clotting factor administered, so they all stood around intently watching the hematologist prepare and infuse the medication.

We were discharged within a few days, a normal time-frame for a typical childbirth, but the whole experience was surreal. It definitely hadn't seemed normal to us, as we had a lot on our minds. And there was a lot more ahead for us to learn.

Show Me the Money

A few weeks later, after settling into new routines and learning to handle a newborn with a chronic illness, our world was turned upside-down once again. Although the diagnosis was a shock, it was nothing compared to the $50,000 bill we got in the mail. This was the first time we realized that life was going to be difficult from then on. Hemophilia we could handle. This we could not.

Obviously it was a mistake, my wife and I both thought. But the insurance company was adamant. Because the NICU was not "in-network," we were responsible for the bill ourselves. How could the NICU not be in-network when the hospital was? The NICU was just down the hall from the room we delivered in!

Nope. The hospital actually subcontracted the NICU out to a third-party provider. This third-party provider was apparently not part of any insurance company's "network." It was a sneaky little trick to help the insurance companies avoid paying out large claims for babies who needed to spend time in the NICU.

In the years since, when I've recounted our story, I've

heard several other people in other parts of the country tell how they experienced the same scenario. Some of them took out second mortgages to pay off the bill.

We decided to fight it. We felt that since we had made our best effort to use an in-network doctor at an in-network hospital, we shouldn't be responsible for the NICU bill. Over a year later, the insurance company finally took responsibility for the bill.

Just Because You Play by the Rules Doesn't Mean You Can Win

Before my son was born, my general impression of insurance companies was that they functioned to keep us as healthy as possible. After Thomas was born, we quickly realized that they are focused more on shareholder value than on improving health. The in-network doctors weren't necessarily the best in town. They were simply the ones who agreed to the insurance company's reduced payment rates.

We made the "choices" that the insurance company permitted us to make. We played by the rules. Yet we still were penalized and our son's care was jeopardized because of the "bottom line." Health care decisions should be based on what the doctor and patient determine to be best. We quickly found that those decisions are instead influenced and controlled by what is best for the insurance companies' balance sheet.

Because of high claims, my employer could no longer shop around for health insurance. No other insurance company would offer my employer a plan, and legally they didn't have to. Before, if premiums rose too high, my employer could shop around and select from several plans based on cost/benefit analysis. Now, we were stuck in one plan forever, forced to accept increased cost, increased cost shifting to employees, reduced benefits, and a new $1 million lifetime cap that kicked my son off in a little over a year.

Until the walls came tumbling down, we were like most Americans, thinking that our health insurance was worth something. That was only because we didn't use it. You don't find out how worthless it is until you actually need it. What we have is collective ignorance, or perhaps denial, of the fact that private for-profit health insurance does not work and is not sustainable. Only through the gift of our son did we finally realize that the emperor has no clothes.

Fighting to Maintain Access to Care

We are indebted to our local Hemophilia Treatment Center for the wonderful care Thomas has received over the past four years. Without the center's comprehensive treatment program, including doctors, nurses, a social worker, and a physical therapist, Thomas would be dealing with some very significant complications today. Thankfully, he is a happy, healthy four-year-old.

As we knew we were going to lose insurance for him (in itself a shocking indictment of our current system), we explored every alternative. Every family at my employer was now dealing with the effects of my son's illness on their high rates and reduced benefits. It was unlikely that I would be able to switch jobs without creating the same impact and jeopardizing my future and that of those around me.

We explored Medicaid, but Thomas could only potentially qualify through a waiver program. There was also no guarantee that he would get the waiver or be able to keep it. We were told that the waiting list for the waiver program was about five years long.

Ultimately, our decision was to start our own business and take advantage of guaranteed-issue insurance in the small group insurance market. That also meant that I had complete control over which insurance company and what benefits package we selected.

Unfortunately, not every plan would allow us to keep the level of care that has enabled Thomas to reach his maximum potential. Many insurance companies would force us to obtain the clotting factor medication from specialty pharmacies influenced by the insurance company. Some plans would lock us into an HMO and make it difficult or impossible to see our current doctor-nurse team. It was obvious that although I could pick the plan, it was still the insurance company that was ultimately in control of treatment decisions and had control over the clinicians making treatment plans. The insurance and plan I selected still had a list of "in-network" providers and coverage limitations.

Choice of Insurance or Choice of Doctors?

Recent health care marketing research shows that people want "choice" in health care and "consumer choice" is a good phrase to use in message framing. It doesn't matter if you are healthy or sick right now. *A choice of limited insurance plans is not a choice at all.* The only way we can get true choice in this country is to move to a single-payer system. Once we do, then we can go to any doctor or hospital we choose. Instead of making our selection based on "who is in," we will make our selection based on "who is best."

Instead of doctors competing for privately insured patients over Medicare and Medicaid patients because of higher payment rates, doctors would simply be competing for patients based on quality and performance measures. Without the insurance companies stepping in between patients and providers, we can return to an era where the doctor-patient team is responsible for treatment decisions.

Who Really Controls Treatment Decisions?

Under today's system, an insurance company employee a thousand miles away with no medical training and no knowledge of the patient history or best medical practices can deny any claim. Thomas was recently denied a prescription that his doctor ordered to help prevent his condition from worsening to the level it was three years ago. Their reason was that it was an "off-label" use, which allowed them to reject any use of a drug that the FDA did not explicitly certify, even if there is good clinical evidence about its benefits. It took several appeals by our medical team and reams of documentation showing that without it, a medical reversal of what took over $2 million in medication to fix might occur. Eventually, they agreed and allowed the prescription to be filled according to the doctor's wishes.

The phrase "consumer-driven health care" is a euphemism for consumer-*paid* health care. My employer was forced to switch to a high-deductible health plan as a result of our increased claims. It meant that in addition to paying an insurance premium, everyone covered under the plan was also paying the first $6,000 of any medical care each year out of his or her own pocket. Co-workers were avoiding going to the doctor for sprained ankles and sore throats. They were getting friends to give them stitches instead of going to the emergency room because they didn't have the money to cover the ER visit. Instead of consumer-driven health care that forces patients to neglect preventive care and treatment, we need patient-centered health care—where the true needs of the patient are served and the doctor-patient relationship is restored.

In a single-payer system, patients would have free choice of doctors, hospitals, and pharmacies. Don't all of us, not just those who are healthy and can afford it, deserve to be able to truly shop around for health care in a transparent market? This will be possible only in a single-payer system.

6

It will let doctors and nurses focus on patients, not paperwork

I. Nursing—by Rose Ann DeMoro

I am sick and tired of watching my patients fight their illnesses and [have to] fight their insurance companies at the same time.

> —Zenei Triunfo-Cortez, Member of the Council of Presidents, California Nurses Association/NNOC

If the United States doesn't take decisive action soon [and guarantee] healthcare to every resident, we'll essentially [become] a Third World country . . . the future of our children and their children is going to be horrific [and] only the elite will have healthcare.

> —Jackie Killeen, Registered Nurse (RN) at Kaiser Permanente

Nurses are on the front lines of the health care battle every day and see the devastating effects of our for-profit health care system. Daily, nurses see patients who have put off preventive medical care because of prohibitive deductibles

---

Rose Ann DeMoro is the Executive Director of the California Nurses Association/National Nurses Organizing Committee.

and co-pays and who then show up in the emergency room with a heart attack triggered by untreated high blood pressure or kidney failure from poorly controlled diabetes. Nurses see the uninsured who delay treatment and are consigned to using the emergency room as a primary care provider. Nurses see people in great need who are denied lifesaving procedures because someone in a distant and impersonal insurance office deems it to be unnecessary, too expensive, or "experimental."

The U.S. health care system in which nurses practice is inefficient, expensive, and unable to meet the health needs of most Americans. Further, our health care system has markedly limited the ways in which nurses deliver care to their patients. These changes have resulted in less direct nursing contact with patients and have increased the patient-to-nurse ratios. Registered nurses increasingly find themselves being replaced by nursing technicians (unlicensed nurses) who are less costly substitutes for nurses at the bedside. Additionally, nurses are inundated with increased paperwork and other bureaucratic responsibilities that consume more nursing time, leaving less time for patients. The traditional nursing roles—delivering care, patient advocacy, and patient education—have been severely hampered because our for-profit health care system is more interested in making money than in providing high-quality health care to patients.

Changes in traditional nursing roles have occurred largely because hospitals implemented cost-containment measures that reflected the rapidly growing privatization of health care in the 1990s. These changes occurred with the increased corporatization of medical care and the drive for increased revenues and profits at the expense of patient care. Subsequent studies have established that these cuts in care standards, including higher patient workloads, created a new shortage of bedside nurses to provide direct patient care and contributed to reductions in quality of patient care.[1] Reductions in nurse staffing levels in hospitals and nursing homes have substantially limited nurses' opportunities to spend sufficient time with their patients. When nurses are unable to monitor, assess, and evaluate their patients at regular intervals, medical complications associated with inpatient stays such as pneumonia, urinary tract infections, bedsores, and postoperative infections have increased.[2] A study reported in the *Journal of the American Medical Association* concluded that "in hospitals with high patient-to-nurse ratios, surgical patients experience higher risk-adjusted 30-day mortality and failure-to-rescue rates, and nurses are more likely to experience burnout and job dissatisfaction."[3]

Although at first glance it may not seem necessary for RNs to check a patient's blood pressure, record vital signs (temperature, respiration rates, and heart rate), or bathe or feed a patient, these were traditionally the very patient-nurse interactions that nurses used as opportunities to clinically assess a patient. Is the patient in more pain? Is the patient more confused today? Is the patient developing a bedsore? Can the patient function independently and go home as scheduled? These are essential questions of good nursing practice. When hospitals reduce a patient's length of stay, nurses are required to care for sicker patients in fewer days. Now, a patient's tests, treatments, and rehabilitation that previously took place over a seven-day period are compressed into three to four days. Thus, a "patient day" now involves more work being done by fewer nurses and less-skilled staff.[4] Hospitalized patients and their families have also noticed these changes and are concerned about the care provided in hospitals. More than 65 percent of Americans believe that an "RN shortage affects their own health and the quality of patient care."[5]

The nation's largest union of registered nurses, the California Nurses Association/National Nurses Organizing Committee (CNA/NNOC), waged a ten-year battle for the passage of the first state law mandating safe nurse-to-patient ratios in the United States. Their nurses understood that increased nurse-staffing levels not only improved quality of care for hospitalized patients[6] but also enhanced job satisfaction for nurses[7] and contributed to overall cost-savings for hospitals. The nurse-to-patient ratios established by California in 1999 are 1:2 in Intensive Critical Care, Neonatal Intensive Care, Post Anesthesia Recovery, and Labor and Delivery; they are 1:4 in the Emergency Room and Pediatrics and 1:5 on Medical/Surgical Units. Although California remains the only state to have enacted legislation that mandates specific nurse-to-patient ratios, eighteen other states are currently considering legislation to guarantee safe nurse-to-patient ratios and there are two federal initiatives calling for "safe hospital nurse staffing."[8]

Since enacting its staffing ratio law, California has seen a 60 percent increase in RN applications and the number of actively licensed RNs has grown by nearly 10,000 a year, compared to just 3,200 a year prior to the law. The fear that hospitals in California could not afford to increase nursing levels disappeared when nurse retention rates at these hospitals improved. The staffing ratio law actually saves hospitals money because they are no longer replacing and retraining nurses at the former rate. Hospitals spend about $42,000 to replace each general medical/surgical unit RN and $64,000 to replace each specialty RN.[9] Mandated staffing levels also provided a better working environment for nurses, which in turn provided hospitalized patients with better nursing care. The success of mandated nurse-to-patient ratios has been shown to reduce risks of hospital-related infections, improve patient outcomes, and result in shorter hospitalizations.[10]

As patients know, nurses have a vital role in combating pain and suffering. Their clinical judgment and expertise should be available to all regardless of the cost. They should not be asked to determine who is or is not entitled to nursing care, nor should they be hindered in performing their healing role because a patient is uninsured or under-insured. Nurses should not have to leave a patient's bedside in the emergency room to confer with an insurance company representative to make sure a particular procedure will be covered. Nurses are trained to facilitate the process of health and healing to their patients, and a publicly funded single-payer health care system offers nurses the best opportunity to pursue their profession without regard to ill-conceived economic constraints determined by private for-profit insurance companies. A single-payer-financed health care system would begin to redress the current inequities in a health care system that many in the nursing profession have struggled to change.

If the goal of our health care system is really to provide high-quality, comprehensive health care to all, then the essential role of strong clinical nursing must be recognized and emphasized. With 2.5 million licensed RNs, 80 percent of whom are actively employed in nursing, registered nurses represent the single largest health profession in the United States.[11] In addition to their important work in hospitals and nursing homes, nurses also work in all of the outpatient settings—clinics, doctors' offices, private homes, schools, employee workplaces, and departments of health. They play a crucial role in patient education and in the management of chronic diseases such as asthma, high blood pressure, and diabetes. Unfortunately, our current health care system limits effective nursing care for chronic illnesses because economic incentives are skewed toward treating the acute complications of chronic illnesses—such as a foot amputation for a diabetic—rather than preventing many of these expensive and disabling complications by ensuring ongoing, high-quality nursing care and physician management.

Making it possible for nurses to work collaboratively with physicians is another important part of good health care. There are about 500,000 New Yorkers diagnosed with diabetes and an additional 200,000 who have diabetes but don't know it. The number of people with diabetes has doubled in New York City in the past ten years, as it has in many other regions of the United States, as the rate of obesity has skyrocketed.[12] To better manage patients with diabetes, four hospitals throughout New York City set up diabetes centers, staffed by doctors, nurse educators, nutritionists, and podiatrists, to provide comprehensive diabetes management. The participating patients' health status improved dramatically as they exercised, ate better, and brought their diabetes under control with the guidance and encouragement of the clinical staff. Despite their medical success, three of the four centers have closed because they "lost money."[13] This is a clear example of a failing health care system. Nurses witness intimately the devastating effects of a system that rewards the private insurance market, stints in funding public programs (such as Medicaid, Medicare, and SCHIP), and expects individuals who require health care to understand the complexity of a system that is difficult to comprehend even if you are a health care professional.

As nurses know firsthand, a national single-payer health care system is the only economical and moral way to finance a fair and equitable health delivery system—one that will be accountable and responsive to patients, the community, our public health, and our health professionals. Indeed, it is time to focus on the health of our nation and not simply the economic health of the insurance companies.

II. Doctors—by Claudia Fegan

What does it say about our health care system that the first question a patient is often asked when she calls for an appointment or arrives at the doctor's office is not "How can we help you?" but "What kind of insurance do you have and how are you going to pay for this visit?" One of the

---

Claudia M. Fegan, MD, is the Associate Chief Medical Officer for the Ambulatory and Community Health Network for the Cook County Bureau of Health Services.

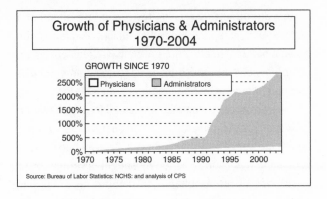

Growth of Physicians & Administrators 1970-2004

GROWTH SINCE 1970

☐ Physicians   ▨ Administrators

2500%
2000%
1500%
1000%
500%
0%
1970 1975 1980 1985 1990 1995 2000

Source: Bureau of Labor Statistics: NCHS: and analysis of CPS

best arguments in favor of national health insurance is that it would allow physicians to return to being physicians focusing on patient care without having to spend so much time trying to figure out who will pay for each test—if needed tests are even covered—or what health insurance network a patient is in. The current system has undermined the professionalism of medical care in this country to such an extent that it is not uncommon for patients to think of their primary care doctor as a gatekeeper whose job it is to block them from needed medical care rather than their advocate whose role it is to fight to provide excellent clinical care. This distortion of the role of the primary care provider has corrupted the doctor-patient relationship.

As a result of our profit-driven health care system, medical decisions are too often driven by the bottom line instead of by patients' medical needs. While the current system discourages screening tests, and furthermore will often refuse coverage altogether for pre-existing conditions, a national health care program would encourage a comprehensive approach to care including an emphasis on prevention. I once had a patient with a history of Barrett's esophagus, a premalignant lesion for which regular monitoring is recommended. Unfortunately, the patient's health insurance had changed when he switched jobs, as is usual in this country. When he sought coverage for an endoscopy of his esophagus to monitor his condition, the insurance company refused coverage, citing its policy of not providing medical coverage for any pre-existing condition. He was thus consigned to wait for the possible development of symptomatic esophageal cancer, a painful and often fatal disease.

As I have seen firsthand time and again, U.S. health care places more emphasis on seeing high patient volume than on the quality of care given at each visit. Too often patients have only a few minutes with their doctor, even if they have multiple complex chronic illnesses. In addition, the average length of time a patient stays in any given private health insurance plan has dropped to less than two years. That is hardly enough time for a physician to get to know a patient, understand his problems, and recognize his needs. While it is common for patients to have the same physician for many years in other industrialized nations, it is the exception in the United States, where each health insurance plan has a different roster of physicians. The quality of each encounter with a physician who barely knows us is diminished and there is no incentive for long-term preventive care or early detection of illness.

The critical skill and medical challenge for primary care physicians is to listen to a patient's medical history and symptoms, analyze them, and make an accurate diagnosis. Ironically, the health insurance reimbursement system favors expensive surgical procedures rather than encouraging and rewarding the cognitive, sometimes time-consuming work to make a thoughtful diagnosis. As a result, fewer and fewer doctors choose primary care.

Some years back a new patient came to see me as she was making some changes in her life. She had just freed herself from a long-term relationship with a man who was a drug addict. I asked her if she had any drug or alcohol dependencies, as it is quite common for people who are in such relationships to abuse various substances together. She denied any substance abuse.

However, her abnormal blood tests reinforced my concern that she might have a problem with alcohol; her blood cells were larger than usual and I suspected liver disease. When I called her and asked again about substance use and she again denied it, I encouraged her to call me in the future if she ever had a problem or wanted to talk to me. A few weeks later her call came. She told me that she was coming out of a four-day drunk and that she was indeed an alcoholic, but after this last episode she wanted to give it up. I told her she was making the right decision and we could get her help. Now the real frustration began. I had to determine her insurance status and have my office staff investigate how to get insurance approval for alcohol detox. Rather than sending the patient to the detox program where she would get the best care or to a specialist I know, I have to send the patient wherever her insurance company dictates.

For-profit insurance companies make money by denying care or by making getting that care unnecessarily difficult. My patient first had to call an 800 number, where she got an answering machine; the message told her to describe her problem on the recorded message and leave a number where she could be reached and that she would receive a call back within twenty-four hours. Those of us who have worked with patients who have problems with substance abuse know that the decision to stop using can be capricious and that patients making this decision are often in a fragile state. It is important to strike while the iron is hot. To expect a patient to describe her problem and her decision to stop using alcohol to an answering machine and then wait for a call back is not only not user-friendly, it can be dangerous. My patient was no exception. She called me back, more than discouraged; she was desolate. I spent more time than I could spare on the phone with her trying to convince her to stick with her decision, and eventually she agreed to try to wait for the call back. The call did not come until noon the next day, nearly twenty-four hours later.

The insurance company directed her to a detox program on the other side of town. By the time my patient arrived there via public transportation a couple of hours later she had been off alcohol for more than twenty-four hours and had developed the sweating and trembling associated with alcohol withdrawal. The intake worker recognized her to be in severe alcohol withdrawal with early DT's (delirium tremens) and she was deemed to be medically unstable and therefore not safe to admit to their program. The worker referred her to the emergency room of the hospital next door. The physician there agreed that the patient was going into DT's, a potentially life-threatening condition. Since his hospital was not in the patient's plan, he called me to get my help transferring the patient to my hospital. The only problem was that my hospital did not have a detox program. She would have to be admitted for DT's, treated, and discharged in order to return again and try to be admitted to the program across town. I implored the emergency department physician to look at the woman in front of him not simply as a diagnosis, as we all do so often, but instead as a human being in need of help. I suggested that he give her an injection of a sedative like librium to relieve her symptoms of alcohol withdrawal and make it possible for her to safely get through the intake process next door, where she could be admitted for her alcoholism and begin the appropriate treatment, and fortunately he agreed. She was admitted to the detox program and for the next four years that she was my patient she remained sober, not because of her insurance program but because two physicians had navigated around considerable obstacles and treated her as a patient in need instead of just another "covered life."

Ours is neither a system designed to meet the needs of the individual nor one that cares whether this patient received the best medical care available. It is a system designed to be the most cost effective for the insurance industry it supports. It is a system that is designed to protect the investments of the stockholders who invest in the insurance industry, not the lives of the patients it covers. As Dr. Arnold Relman wrote in his recent book on health care reform, *A Second Opinion,* "the contrast between the economic success of the corporations that derive their income from the health care system and the pain that the system is inflicting on the rest of us produces growing unrest."

There is a common misconception that our profit-driven health care system promotes innovation in medicine. This ignores the fact that the largest sources of funding for medical research in the United States are public sources such as the National Institutes of Health (NIH) and public universities. It also conveniently ignores all of the innovations that have come from countries with universal health care, such as the first heart-lung transplant and the first laparoscopic cholecystectomy, both of which were first performed in Canada. Although people think that pharmaceutical companies are responsible for new and innovative medications, the reality is that most of what the pharmaceutical industry funds in this country is the development of "me-too" medications for drugs developed already by the NIH. Of 2,871 new medications approved by the Food and Drug Administration (FDA) in the United States between 1981 and 2003, only seven drugs were a new molecular entity that offered a new therapy not previously provided by another medication.

Rather than stimulating innovation, the competition created by market forces smothers it. Increasingly, medical researchers in universities are told they need to see more patients and spend less time in the lab in order to pay for their salaries. We are pushing a system that has become so dollar driven that we can't pay people to think and come up with new ideas. Why? Because it is too difficult to quantify thinking and no one wants to pay for something that can't be quantified. If you check a patient's stool, find blood, order a colonoscopy, and find and remove a premalignant polyp—thus preventing colon cancer—the bulk of the reimbursement goes to the colonoscopist who removes the polyp. There is no compensation for remembering to check the stool, ordering the colonoscopy, and thereby preventing the colon cancer. American health care is focused on compensating for procedures and not on cognitive efforts to keep patients well.

What we need is a system that pays for health care for everyone, is not dependent on employment, and allows physicians to take care of the patient in front of them without concern about how the patient will pay for it. Such a system will allow us to re-establish the critical concept of continuity of medical care, allowing the patient to develop a relationship with a primary care provider over a period of years, not months. The physicians, in turn, will get the chance to know patients as individuals, learn their medical histories, and recognize when something is serious and needs immediate attention or when watchful waiting is appropriate. National health insurance would allow physicians to once again be physicians thinking in terms of patients rather than reimbursable service. It is time we recognized that market forces have failed to work in medicine; they have failed to control costs, because patients don't know enough about health care to recognize quality care. It is time that physicians have the chance to maximize that quality care instead of being forced to focus on maximizing productivity and profit. It is time to remember the reason we went to medical school in the first place.

7

It will reduce health care disparities

Olveen Carrasquillo and Jaime Torres

Disparities in health insurance coverage must be addressed as an important first step toward eliminating the health care disparities that disproportionately affect the economically disadvantaged and people of color. Examples of such health care disparities include the black infant mortality rate, which at 13.6 infant deaths per 1,000 live births is double that of non-Hispanic whites (NHWs) at 5.7.[1] Another example is diabetes; 13 percent of Hispanics and 15 percent of black adults have diabetes versus 8 percent of NHWs.[2] The causes of these health disparities are complex and multifactorial and include issues related to the environment, poverty, housing, education, health behaviors, and even segregation and discrimination. Another important contributor to these health care disparities is the difference in

Olveen Carrasquillo, MD, MPH, is an Associate Professor of Medicine, Health Policy and Community Partnerships at Columbia University Medical Center. Jaime Torres, DPM, MS, is the founder and president of Latinos for National Health Insurance.

quality of the health care received by racial or ethnic minorities versus that of NHWs. Examples of these health care disparities include blacks' receiving fewer bypass surgeries and kidney transplants than NHWs. Although blacks are one and a half times more likely to die from heart disease than whites, the rate of bypass surgery among whites was 9 per 1,000 versus 4 per 1,000 among blacks in 2001.[3] Similarly, while over 50 percent of NHWs have received age-appropriate colorectal cancer screening, only 35 percent of Asians and Hispanics have had such tests.[4]

In 1999, Congress commissioned the Institute of Medicine (IOM) to produce an in-depth report on health care disparities. The charge was to examine the existence of disparities that were not due to known factors such as health insurance coverage and ability to pay. What the IOM found was that even after accounting for insurance, members of racial and ethnic minorities received lower-quality health care than NHWs. Yet, as this landmark report points out, disentangling the impact of known causes of disparities, such as access to affordable health insurance, from broader economic and social inequities is an "artificial and difficult distinction." The IOM noted that while disparities in access to affordable quality health care are "likely the most significant barrier to equitable care," other factors such as bias, discrimination, and negative racial stereotypes are also important barriers to equitable care. Additional contributors to health care disparities included cultural and linguistic barriers, lack of a stable primary care clinician, and fragmentation of the health care system.

The annual statistics published by the Census Bureau portray a dismal picture of health insurance coverage among minorities.[5] The data show that one-third of Latinos in the United States lack health insurance coverage and 20 percent of both blacks and Asians in the United States are uninsured as well. In contrast, only 10 percent of NHWs are uninsured. Further, from 1987 to 2005, the proportion of the uninsured population in the United States that is minority has increased from 42 percent to 53 percent.[6] Among Latinos and Asians, the most vulnerable are immigrants. Over half of noncitizen Latinos and nearly a third of noncitizen Asians in the United States lack health coverage. It also estimated that nearly 80 percent of undocumented immigrants lack insurance. However, even U.S.-born Latinos (over 60 percent of all Latinos are U.S. born) are twice as likely as NHWs to lack coverage. Thus, immigration status by itself does not explain a large proportion of the disparities in health coverage between minorities and NHWs in the United States.

Medical Apartheid in the United States

In the absence of a system of universal health care, a multi-tier health care system has developed in the United States, one that results in what can be described as health care segregation. In the highest tier are those who have private insurance coverage, usually through their employer or Medicare. These insurance programs are widely accepted by physicians and hospitals. At the other end are the uninsured. In theory, they can pay for their health care services out of pocket. In reality, as most of the uninsured are either poor or middle class, they often forgo necessary care. Their alternative is to rely on a safety net patchwork of providers including community health centers, outpatient departments of public and some not-for-profit hospitals, and emergency rooms. While an important source of care for the uninsured, such patched-together systems are a far cry from the care received by privately insured and Medicare populations. In particular, access to subspecialty care and a stable source of outpatient medications are major barriers to care in these safety-net systems. While 85 percent of NHWs in this country belong to the highest tier of health care, only 63 percent of blacks and 50 percent of Hispanics belong to this top tier of access (see Figure 7.1). Further, while racial and ethnic minorities make up less than a third of the U.S. population, over half of all persons in this lowest tier of health care are minorities.

In the middle tier are those covered through the various insurance programs serving the poor such as Medicaid and the State Children's Health Insurance Programs (SCHIP). These programs are critical components of the

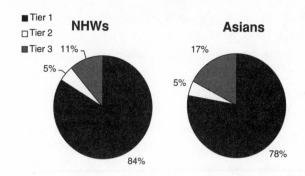

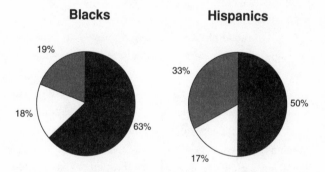

Figure 7.1. **Medical Apartheid in the United States**

Tier 1= Medicare and private plans

Tier 2= Segregated care through Medicaid and SCHIP

Tier 3= Uninsured

health care safety net and cover 40 million children and adults. Unfortunately, as is true for most other poverty programs, they suffer chronic underfunding and applicants face onerous eligibility and recertification requirements. In some states, over half of all persons who enroll are disenrolled in under a year. Further, when facing budgetary difficulties, limiting enrollment in these programs or rationing health care services through cutbacks of services covered is a favorite ploy of many legislators. Thus, for many enrollees, such programs are a far cry from the comprehensive, ongoing health care access that persons in the first tier enjoy.

The real reason that these underfunded programs are segregated is that in most states providers are paid at levels much lower than Medicare. As an example, in New York a private physician can be paid six times more to see a patient with Medicare versus Medicaid. As a result, fewer than half of all providers nationally choose to accept Medicaid patients. In many localities, this forces most Medicaid patients to receive care through the same network of safety net clinics that exist for the uninsured. Further, access to subspecialty care in these settings is often as problematic as it is with the uninsured. As an example, in one large hospital in New York City, the wait for a Medicaid patient to see a gastroenterologist is eight months. In contrast, a patient with Medicare could be seen within two weeks in the private offices that are part of the same medical center but do not accept Medicaid patients. The government also reinforces this segregated system of care, because it provides additional subsidies or grants for designated safety net providers and clinics to see Medicaid patients but does not make such funds available to providers in private practice. This segregationist system is quite effective at ensuring that those in the first tier receive a different level of care from those in the second and third tiers. A report by one advocacy coalition, Bronx Reach Coalition, extensively described this system of segregated care and unequal access faced by poor and predominantly minority patients as "Medical Apartheid."[7] Among the report's conclusions were that people who are uninsured or publicly insured (through Medicaid, Medicaid Managed Care, Family Health Plus, and Child Health Plus) are often cared for in separate institutions from those who are privately insured. The coalition also found that even within health care institutions, separate and unequal systems of care exist. The uninsured, people covered by Medicaid, and sometimes even those enrolled in Medicaid Managed Care, Family Health Plus, and Child Health Plus receive poorer care in different locations, at different times, and by less-trained physicians than those who are privately insured. Finally, the report shows that when patients are sorted according to their insurance status, this segregated care leads to different health outcomes.

Can One Size Possibly Fit All?

Other chapters in this book have discussed the limitations of the market-based solutions espoused by most Republicans, whose central premise is that health care is a commodity and should be distributed based on ability to pay. Such market-based initiatives would clearly widen the gap in health and health care between the haves and have-nots in our society. This is not a Republican-versus-Democrat problem, however. Almost as troubling are the Democratic approaches that call for placing most low-income uninsured persons into safety-net health insurance programs such as Medicaid. When pressed on the issue, many Democrats agree that a system that provides equitable, comprehensive coverage would go a long way toward addressing health disparities. Yet they usually then cite vague terms such as "political feasibility" and "compromise" and some not-so-vague terms such as "powerful opposition" to explain why they favor approaches that would institutionalize apartheid and discrimination in health care. In fact, they are willing to champion a racist system of health care rather than stand up to the pharmaceutical and for-profit health insurance industries.

In contrast, under a comprehensive national health insurance plan, a wealthy NHW male would have the same level of coverage as a low-income black female. Detractors claim that this one-size-fits-all approach is not consistent with American values and that individuals should have the freedom to choose the level and quality of health care they wish to receive. However, such detractors have a hard time identifying persons who would want to receive low-quality health care. Clearly, under the mantra of choice, it would be minorities who would disproportionately be stuck in the lowest levels of health care. From a perspective of basic fairness, it is clear that having one system of care in which access to high-quality health care would be a right of all is far superior to one in which quality of coverage is determined by income.

Does Everyone in and No One out Include All Immigrants?

Immigrants contribute tens of billions of dollars to our economy, and the sustainability of programs such as Social Security and Medicare to a significant extent depends on taxes paid by such workers. Further, health costs for immigrants are about one-third those of NHWs. Ethical, religious, and humane issues could all be raised to support improving access to care for such immigrants. However, the main reason all immigrants would be included in national health insurance (NHI) is financial. Not only are immigrants relatively inexpensive to cover, but to exclude them would mean maintenance of very expensive administrative systems of billing and indirect and inefficient safety-net reimbursement mechanisms. Simply put, NHI would be much more costly if a system needs to be maintained to exclude 12 million undocumented persons. Thus, comprehensive coverage of all residents of the United States would be far more humane *and* less costly.

Political and Organizational Support for NHI among Minorities

Since NHI is the only proposal for universal coverage that would ensure equitable high-quality health care for all, it has long been supported by the Congressional Black Caucus. Over half the members of the Congressional Hispanic Caucus also support HR 676. NHI also enjoys support among large minority medical groups such as the National Medical Association and the National Hispanic Medical Association. In response, the strategy favored by the insurance and pharmaceutical industries has been to partner with minority political leaders and organizations on other important disparities issues such as workforce diversity, cultural competency, and language barriers—but not on NHI. By lavishing groups with funding for other initiatives, these opponents of single payer hope not only to gain the goodwill of these political leaders and organizations but also to divert advocacy on behalf of NHI. Fortunately, so far this approach has had limited success, with the majority of minority leaders and organizations remaining strong advocates of NHI.

Will NHI end disparities? No. Health disparities are an extremely complex and multifaceted problem that has long plagued our society. As we've said earlier, disparities in health are due to a variety of factors—including environment, housing, poverty, education, and racism—that go far beyond just having insurance. Indeed, even in countries that have universal coverage, the wealthy and privileged enjoy better health status and find ways to receive better access to care than those in poverty. However, the magnitude of health care disparities in those countries is significantly less than in the United States. Many of us believe that once we have enacted a system of equitable, comprehensive coverage for all, we can then focus on addressing other important issues. These include ensuring a health care workforce whose diversity is reflective of our society, health care providers who are culturally and linguistically competent to provide care to persons from a wide variety of racial and ethnic backgrounds, and a health care delivery system that is free of the many racial and ethnic biases and stereotypes that plague our society. But since disparities in access to quality health care are a major contributor to disparities in health, health insurance is the key driver of many health care disparities, and efforts to address disparities must start with the most glaring and obvious factor.

8

It will eliminate medical debt

Cindy Zeldin and Mark Rukavina

Health care is one of the top domestic issues for Americans. The cost of health care continues to rise sharply, outpacing overall inflation and wage growth and adding pressure to already stretched family budgets. Health spending now accounts for 16 percent of our nation's gross domestic product, up from 13.8 percent in 2000.[1] Over the past six years, health insurance premiums have increased by more than six times the median income (73.8 percent versus 11.6 percent).[2] As low- and middle-income Americans try to secure health care for their families, these spiraling costs are landing many households in the red.

The number of Americans without health insurance coverage grew by more than 2 million between 2005 and 2006, with 47 million Americans—just under 16 percent of the population—having no coverage.[3] The vast majority of Americans with health insurance have coverage through their own or a family member's workplace.[4] However, as

Cindy Zeldin is a health policy researcher with nearly a decade of public policy experience at the state and national levels. Mark Rukavina is the Executive Director of the Access Project.

employers look to rein in benefit costs, workers are experiencing a decrease in the value of the insurance. Employers are selecting insurance policies that require greater employee cost sharing through higher deductibles, co-payments, and other forms of out-of-pocket expenses.[5] Some employers are eliminating coverage altogether. Sixty percent of American businesses offered coverage to their employees in 2007, a dramatic drop from 69 percent in the year 2000.[6]

As the 2008 presidential candidates propose solutions to address the lack of health insurance for 47 million Americans, attention must be paid to the quality of health insurance coverage offered them. Many insured Americans are feeling financially burdened by health care costs. It is estimated that more than 45 million Americans live in households where more than 10 percent of after-tax family income is being spent on insurance premiums and out-of-pocket health care expenses.[7]

It is well established that uninsured Americans do not have equal access to health care. They are also particularly vulnerable to medical bill problems and to medical debt.[8] Unfortunately, such struggles are far from limited to the uninsured. A recent national survey found that a quarter of Americans have medical bills or medical debts that they are paying off over time and among this group over two-thirds have health insurance.[9] Numerous studies have found that large numbers of both insured and uninsured

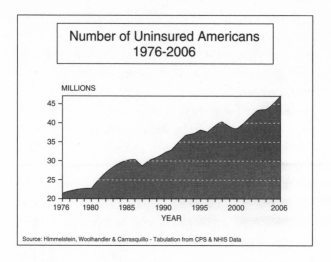

Number of Uninsured Americans
1976-2006

MILLIONS

Source: Himmelstein, Woolhandler & Carrasquillo - Tabulation from CPS & NHIS Data

Americans have difficulty paying medical bills and are even falling into debt.[10]

Simply stated, medical debt is a growing problem with severe consequences for both access to necessary health care services and financial stability. Studies have documented that adults with medical debt, whether insured or uninsured, are more likely than those without debt to skip recommended treatments, leave drug prescriptions unfilled, and postpone care because of cost.[11] Roughly half of all personal bankruptcies are due in part to medical problems.[12] Even relatively small levels of medical debt can have major consequences on financial security.[13]

To meet out-of-pocket medical expenses, many patients are turning to credit in order to avoid owing money directly to the providers of their care. Late in 2007, investigative journalists uncovered lending practices that were considered predatory by some experts. Practices uncovered included offers too good to be true such as zero percent interest health credit cards. Many patients saw their interest rate skyrocket to more than 25 percent with one late payment. Some patients were charged excessive fees for the services they received, and the interest on those fees resulted in patients' struggling to make the minimum monthly payment; still others were dunned by collection agencies using aggressive tactics to extract payment from people without available cash to pay their unexpected medical bills. The documentation of such tactics prompted Senator Charles Grassley (R-Iowa), ranking member of the Senate Finance Committee, to state, "I'm very troubled by what we're seeing with some nonprofit hospitals' cozying up to banks, debt buyers, and credit-card companies over patients' medical bills."[14]

Using a credit card for medical expenses is especially pernicious because it subjects patients to high interest rates, harsh late fees, and penalties. To gain a better understanding of this phenomenon, Demos and The Access Project partnered to analyze data from Demos's national household survey of low- and moderate-income households with credit card debt. Included in this survey were

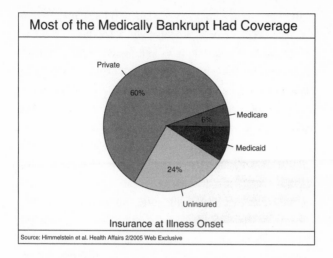

Most of the Medically Bankrupt Had Coverage

Private 60%

Medicare 6%

Medicaid

24%

Uninsured

Insurance at Illness Onset

Source: Himmelstein et al. Health Affairs 2/2005 Web Exclusive

questions about medical expenses as a component of credit card debt and health insurance status. The results, which we reproduce in summary form in the remainder of this chapter, were published in a 2006 report jointly released by Demos and The Access Project entitled "Borrowing to Stay Healthy."[15]

Our findings show that low- and middle-income households who cited medical expenses as a factor in their credit card debt had higher levels of credit card debt than those who did not cite this factor. Overall in the survey, nearly one in three (29 percent) of low- and middle-income households with credit card debt reported that medical expenses contributed to their current level of credit card debt. Within that group, the vast majority (69 percent) had a major medical expense in the previous three years. Overall, one in five (20 percent) of indebted low- and middle-income households reported having a major medical expense in the previous three years and that medical expenses contributed to their current level of credit card debt. Within this "medically indebted" group, we found that over half (57 percent) had credit card debt higher than $5,000, with the vast majority of them having credit card debt higher than $10,000. Average credit card debt was also far higher for low- and middle-income medically indebted households as compared to households who neither had a recent major medical expense nor cited medical expenses as contributing to their credit card debt. For households with medical debt on their credit cards, average credit card debt was higher for those without health insurance. Medical debt can seriously threaten both financial well-being and access to health care services. The low- to middle-income households in our survey showed many signs of financial stress: a majority of them cited having been called by bill collectors, and one in seven (15 percent) had declared bankruptcy.

Our report also discussed the rise of medical credit cards and loans and how these products fit into the picture for patients with medical debt. To help place these lending products into context, let us first discuss the many health insurance gaps that created the opening for them.

In part to stem the growth of health insurance premiums, more insurers and employers are offering insurance plans that feature higher levels of cost sharing, potentially exposing low- and moderate-income patients to financial stress.

Holes in health insurance plans include medications, procedures, and medical equipment excluded from coverage, higher rates of cost sharing for out-of-network providers, and multiple deductibles.[16] More than a fifth of workers are in insurance plans without an out-of-pocket maximum and about half of workers are in health insurance plans with a lifetime benefit maximum.[17] When illness strikes, these gaps often result in crushing medical debt. Of course, the 47 million Americans without any health insurance face the greatest risk. Despite the common perception that the uninsured receive free care in the emergency room setting, there is considerable evidence not only that the uninsured face negative health consequences as a result of being uninsured[18] but also that many patients without health insurance are still billed for services; in fact, because they don't receive the same discounts that insurers negotiate for their members, the uninsured are often billed the full "sticker price" for health care services, landing them in debt to health providers or to the creditors to whom their debt is turned over.

It is estimated that in 2007 Americans spent $265 billion on out-of-pocket health care costs; this is in addition to what they spent on health insurance premiums. This is a tempting amount for creditors who view these costs as a new market niche. A *Business Week* investigation in late 2007 documented an array of credit cards and lending products that have emerged in recent years to capitalize on out-of-pocket medical expenses that exceed patients' ability to pay. In some cases, medical providers were signing up patients unable to pay their medical bills for a medical credit card without their full understanding of the credit terms, leaving these patients with large bills quickly accruing interest.

Many medical providers are looking for new ways to manage their accounts receivable. Partnering with fiscal intermediaries, facilitating connections with lenders, and contracting with collection agencies are becoming quite common. Increasingly, medical providers are looking to sell their accounts to debt buyers who are quite interested in this market, especially given its size.[19] Unfortunately for consumers, such transactions can result in serious consequences as unaffordable medical bills are transformed into delinquent accounts and reported to the credit bureaus.

Policymakers must address the twin problems of rising health care costs and eroding coverage in a comprehensive manner to protect American families from the financial insecurity and deleterious health outcomes that can result from medical debt. Policymakers should pursue an approach that provides universal, affordable access to comprehensive benefits without exposing patients and their families to the burden of medical debt.

9

It will be good for labor and for business

Leo W. Gerard

A System in Crisis

Today the nation is faced with a private/public health care financing system that has left one-third of the American people with either inadequate health insurance or no coverage at all. Forty-nine percent of people *with insurance* tell pollsters they are somewhat or completely unprepared to cope with a costly medical emergency over the coming year.[1] Twenty-nine percent of people *with underinsurance* often postpone medical care because of costs, problems compounded by the fact that incomes have been relatively stagnant for active workers and are in decline for those on fixed incomes.[2] Premiums are going up while benefits are going down. Four percent of middle-income families—those earning between $40,000 and $80,000 annually—lost employer-based health insurance between 2000 and 2005.[3] Four percent may sound small, but it represents 2 million families.[4] Half of those families lost their insurance because their employers abandoned health insurance programs; another

Leo W. Gerard is International President of the United Steelworkers.

15 percent lost their insurance because their premiums became unaffordable.

Union negotiators and health care program administrators have spent years pulling rabbits out of hats to compensate for the increasing costs of health care. Introducing generic drugs and preferred provider organizations and raising deductibles and co-pays have all been strategies developed to patch a collapsing system. Despite these "innovations," employers' costs of group health insurance went from $331 billion in 2000 to $514 billion in 2005, or about 9 percent of total wage and salary costs.[5]

Many of today's collective bargaining disputes are driven by health care costs.

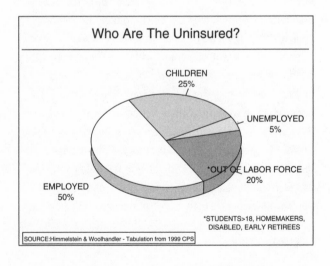

Who Are The Uninsured?

CHILDREN
25%

UNEMPLOYED
5%

*OUT OF LABOR FORCE
20%

EMPLOYED
50%

*STUDENTS>18, HOMEMAKERS,
DISABLED, EARLY RETIREES

SOURCE:Himmelstein & Woolhandler - Tabulation from 1999 CPS

Rather than joining labor to lobby for universal, affordable health care, private employers are abandoning financial responsibility for health care costs at the rate of about 5 percent per year, reducing the number of group plan participants, driving down employee living standards, and further undermining private-sector health care financing.[6] As employer definancing of health care continues unabated, the move to a national system will no longer be a choice; it will be a necessity in order to maintain any health care system whatsoever.

Undermining Global Competitiveness

Employers increasingly point to the disadvantage they suffer when competing globally, especially companies operating in the many nations that have developed uniform, government-supported health care. In those nations, even where financing is derived from both private and public sources, administration of the system and guidelines for care have become publicly supported social services.

In the United States, where financial accounting standards require employers to carry their long-term liabilities for retiree health care on their balance sheets, unions are put in the unenviable but inevitable position of having to press demands for health care benefit coverage in bargaining not only for their existing dues-paying members but also for a considerable number of retirees. Especially in the industrial sectors of the economy, the number of retirees whose interests must be represented often far exceeds the number of active members, as was the case with United Steelworkers (USW) negotiations with the Goodyear Tire and Rubber Company and more recently in the United Automobile Workers' negotiations with the auto industry.

It is little wonder, then, that in negotiations with these companies, unions have felt compelled by the twin goals of preserving and securing retiree benefits and keeping employers competitive to negotiate Voluntary Employee Benefits Associations (VEBAs), trusts funded by the companies and administered by boards of trustees independent of the employer. Because their assets will be immune from any potential bankruptcy of the employer, these VEBAs provide continuing and secured health care benefits for current and future retirees while lifting a significant body of health care liabilities that employers are obliged to carry on their books. And their assets can be increased through contributions negotiated in future contract bargaining. No competitor of General Motors or Goodyear elsewhere in the industrialized world carries such liabilities or obligations, as all are beneficiaries of health care subsidized by their governments in one fashion or another. Only in the United States must these obligations be secured through collective bargaining if workers and retirees are to have any hope of receiving health care benefits. (The value of securing such benefits is of course not lost on those workers who have enjoyed health care coverage only to see it wiped out by their employers' bankruptcies.)

Cruel Irony

That retired union members should be among those most victimized by the nation's health care crisis is cruelly ironic, for the origins of America's current health care financing system are rooted in labor-management collective bargaining agreements forged during World War II. Negotiators introduced enhanced health care benefits as a reward for workers during a period when wage increases were restricted by war policy measures. These benefits soon became a standard part of employment compensation.

The result was a stable financial base for the growth and improvement of health care systems across the nation. Communities had money for hospitals and infrastructure. The medical profession was able to upgrade its capabilities, do more research, and professionalize care. Financing was handled by a growing private insurance industry that was dominated by nonprofit-style carriers. But there was another, less noticed outcome of America's health care evolution. Health care professionals began to enjoy a new upper-middle-class status, and health insurance executives became increasingly acquisitive as they gained control of significant pools of health insurance reserves. Eventually a system that had been nonprofit in character morphed into a for-profit enterprise, with costs spiraling out of control as the health insurance industry became concerned with the bottom line rather than providing a real health care benefit to working Americans.

The Private System's Shortcomings

Rife with inefficiency and shaped by the drive for profit and exorbitant executive compensation, the private financing system is inherently ill-equipped to provide equitable health care for all of America's population, let alone to continue to provide it affordably to workers with a union contract. As the costs of care have increased, often much more rapidly than the rate of inflation, the deficiencies of a system that relies disproportionately on employer-based financing have become more apparent.

The inefficiency and rising costs of the American health care system have ripple effects throughout the economy, affecting not only unions but all Americans. Health care costs impede efforts to reverse the United States' massive trade deficits, which are further eroding competitiveness and well-paying jobs. Our product and service costs are driven up by the refusal to implement an efficient health care system. Some estimates cite the waste in our health care system as representing as much as 7 percent of the nation's productive capacity (gross domestic product).[7] Since we are a debtor nation, these costs flow directly into the national debt and further weaken our national financial strength.

Corporate Blind Mice

The best face that can be put on the unwillingness of corporate executives to abandon our broken system in favor of universal health care is their misbegotten belief that the current system can be stabilized enough to make the costs amenable to effective business planning. Yet, in reality, as things stand today, businesses have no leverage whatsoever over either quality or price. Their only "control" is over the amount of coverage they will pay for—an approach they all too frequently default to in contract negotiations.

A national single-payer system would relieve corporations of the burden of health insurance administration, stabilize costs, and give corporations the global level playing field they want. Businesses can play a major role in solving the health care dilemma, therefore, by overcoming their blind resistance to a national system and insisting instead that a national plan be designed that provides their employees with proper coverage without runaway costs. Universal coverage through a single-payer system offers the best hope of achieving these goals.

It's so simple. Most people who can't afford health insurance are also too poor to owe taxes. But if you give them a deduction from the taxes they don't owe, they can use the money they're not getting back to buy the health care they can't afford.

—Stephen Colbert on the Bush Health Plan

10

It's what most Americans want—and we can make it happen

Joanne Landy and Oliver Fein

The irony about the debate over national health insurance in the United States is that we have excellent hospitals, skilled practitioners, and the technological infrastructure—and we're already spending enough money to insure everyone and to improve access to care for many who are covered today by inadequate plans. All we need is the political will.

Although the barriers to single-payer reform are considerable, we ignore them at our peril. Private, for-profit insurance companies will of course fight tooth and nail against any system that will remove them from a significant role in the country's health care. Big Pharma too will use its clout to try to defeat single payer; the drug companies want multiple fragmented private purchasers rather

Joanne Landy, MPH, MA, is the former executive director of the New York Metro Chapter of Physicians for a National Health Program. Oliver Fein, MD, is a practicing general internist, Professor of Clinical Medicine and Public Health, and Associate Dean at the Weill Cornell Medical College.

than a single public payer with the power to negotiate lower prices for everyone. Moreover, most politicians are, right now, of little help. Too often they take money from and are then beholden to insurance and drug companies. (However, with sufficient popular pressure, many politicians would have to change their stance and could add important strength and credibility to the fight for single payer.) In addition, numerous economists and health care "experts" lend legitimacy to the current system by advocating market-oriented reforms, reforms that fail to be truly universal, and meanwhile pour more money into private insurance companies. Finally, while employers often complain about the high cost of private health insurance premiums, they have thus far chosen to deal with rising premiums by shifting costs to their employees rather than by supporting a public insurance solution.

Overcoming these obstacles will require an informed public that demands meaningful change. The movement for single payer has made great strides, drawing on the fact that most people in this country have come to distrust insurance companies. But many Americans have grown increasingly distrustful of government in recent years. It is not uncommon to hear comments like "You mean you want the government that didn't rescue New Orleans after Katrina to solve the health care crisis? Forget it!" Understandably, those with health insurance fear that they will lose the benefits they have now and that the cost of a government-financed system will mean that they will have to pay extraordinarily high taxes and will end up even worse off than they are now.

However, as the chapters in this book illustrate, the arguments against single payer don't measure up to the evidence. Here are some of the myths that need to be dispelled:

- **Universal coverage costs too much.** No, it doesn't. Every other industrialized nation offers its people universal coverage, and at a cost much lower than we now spend in the United States, which covers only part of its population. In 2005, we spent 15.3 percent of our gross domestic product on health care compared to France's 11.1 percent, Germany's 10.7 percent, and Canada's 9.8 percent.[1] Yet, in 2005 we had 45 million uninsured (it's 2 million more at this writing!) while other industrialized countries covered everyone's health care.

- **Your taxes will go up.** Perhaps, but you are still likely to come out ahead when you consider the overall expenses. Single payer will cost most people the same or less than the premiums and medical bills they are paying today and will be secure regardless of employment or income. Both the Congressional Budget Office and the General Accounting Office have testified that the United States could insure everyone for the amount of money we're spending.[2]

- **Americans get world-class care—we shouldn't mess around with that.** The fact is that many Americans don't get world-class care. Sure, if you are wealthy and have the best private insurance, your chances of getting excellent care are high. But on almost all measures of health care and mortality, we lag behind Canada and Europe.[3]

- **Other countries have much longer waiting times than we do.** In actuality in other industrialized countries there are no waiting lists for emergency surgery or urgently needed procedures. It's true that the United States has shorter waits for elective surgery than Canada and England. But recent studies show that some waiting times in the United States are longer than in other countries. For example, in a study of seven developed countries, the Commonwealth Fund looked at how many sick adults had to wait six days or more for an appointment.[4] By this measure, only Canada's record was worse than ours. Within our market-driven system, an appointment for cosmetic surgery may be scheduled sooner than an appointment for possible skin cancer. A recent study reported an average wait of seventy-three days for patients with possible skin cancer in Boston.[5]

- **There is no problem; people get care even if they're uninsured.** Don't tell that to the American Cancer Society (ACS), which in September 2007 worked with its sister advocacy organization, the ACS Cancer Action Network, to launch a major initiative to make access to health care a state and national priority. Research shows that uninsured patients were much more likely to have their cancers diagnosed at an advanced stage, when they are less curable, than were patients with insurance.[6] John Seffrin, the society's chief executive, has stated that unless the health care system is fixed "lack of access will be a bigger cancer killer than tobacco."[7] Of course the problem isn't limited to cancer: the Institute of Medicine estimates that there are 22,000 deaths per year due to lack of insurance.[8] Unnecessary suffering and disease affect millions more who have no insurance or are underinsured.

- **Single payer is socialized medicine.** Single payer is *not* socialized medicine, because for the most part government will not own the hospitals and physicians will not be on salary to government. Single payer simply changes the financing of health care; the health care delivery system remains the same. It will operate like the Medicare program for the elderly today, in which patients are seen by private doctors in (mostly) private hospitals; this clearly isn't socialized medicine. Single payer is actually "social insurance" rather than "private insurance."

Everyone—including most Democrats and some Republicans—is talking about the need for universal health care coverage and cost controls. Although not everyone endorses single payer at this time, more and more people have jobs with no insurance, and those with insurance are seeing their employers reduce their benefits and increase their contributions for premiums, year by year. The latest General Motors–United Automobile Workers agreement points toward a grim future in which employers try to shed all responsibility for insuring their employees. Meanwhile, every study that compares single payer with tax deductions or tax subsidies to buy private health insurance shows that single payer costs less and guarantees better coverage to more people than all the other approaches.

The evidence supports single payer, and increasing numbers of people in this country are seeing that we don't have to be stuck with the irrational, expensive, and cruel system we have. Michael Moore's *SiCKO!* has made an incalculable contribution to overcoming ignorance about what is possible: Moore has shown us that by cutting the wasteful and totally unnecessary private insurance industry out of our health care system we can have real universal health insurance. Of course there have been vicious attacks on Moore, but the strong positive response to *SiCKO*—from Oprah to the *New York Times* to Jon Stewart—has begun to puncture the traditional U.S. media blackout of the truth about single payer. Perhaps most important, Moore has made a convincing case that government can work for people and has brought outrage and a passion for justice to the fight for a humane health care system in the United States. He is among those helping to ignite the movement needed to make it a reality.

In another hopeful sign, more and more groups are endorsing HR 676. This is the bill in the U.S. House of Representatives introduced by Michigan's John Conyers Jr., called the United States National Health Insurance Act or Expanded and Improved Medicare for All. As of this writing HR 676 has been endorsed by the National Organization for Women, the NAACP, and a wide variety of religious and civil groups, including We Be Illin', a group of young people reaching out to their peers to show why they urgently need single payer. HR 676 has also been endorsed by 401 union organizations in 48 states including 104 Central Labor Councils and Area Labor Federations and 33 state AFL-CIOs (as of April 23, 2008). The AFL-CIO has adopted a policy statement favoring a Medicare-for-All approach. The Alliance of Retired Americans, but not to date the American Association of Retired Persons (AARP), reaffirmed its earlier support for HR 676 in September 2007. It is encouraging that all these groups have indicated their support for HR 676; the next challenge is gaining endorsement from more organizations and enlisting those that have already endorsed to deploy their resources in an active fight to pass the bill and actually bring single payer to fruition.

More and more physicians are coming around to support a single-payer system. Physicians for a National Health Program (www.PNHP.org) has long advocated single-payer national health insurance, and more doctors are coming to agree with them. In a well-designed study of Massachusetts physicians drawn from the American Medical Association (AMA) master file, 62 percent supported single-payer reform.[9] In January 2008, the American College of Physicians, the second largest physician organization in the United States after the AMA, published a position paper recommending "Single-payer financing models, in which one government entity is the sole third-party payer of health care costs," as one pathway to reform.[10] Recently, the New York State Academy of Family Physicians gave testimony strongly endorsing single payer. The AMA does not have the stranglehold on physician opinion that it once had. Its membership has fallen to 27 percent of physicians. The AMA no longer represents the majority of practicing physicians in the United States. Many physicians are furious with the second-guessing and interference by the private insurance industry, which denies claims and delays treatment and payment. Physicians become frustrated and patients suffer when each private insurance company's pharmaceutical formulary is different, so that patients can't get certain medications or have higher co-pays. Private insurance company rules on prior approvals result in delay or denial of patient care. Physicians feel ethically compromised. The physician is ultimately accountable to the patient, whereas the insurance company has a responsibility only to its stockholders to maximize profits.

The majority of the public favor national health insurance. A full 68 percent said in the September 2006 ABC/Kaiser/USA Today poll that "providing health care coverage for all Americans" was more important than "holding down taxes."[11] The more recent CNN/Opinion Research Corporation poll (May 2007) finds similar results. Asked whether the "government should provide a national health insurance program for all Americans even if this would require higher taxes," 64 percent of the sample said yes, while just 35 percent said no. When CNN asked that same question in January 1995, 55 percent answered yes and 37 percent said no. This is not an explicit endorsement of single payer, of course. It does suggest, though, that more than a majority of Americans see government and higher taxes as part of the solution to the health care crisis—even when they have not been informed that lower premiums, deductibles, and co-pays would compensate most people for their higher taxes under a single-payer system.

Halfway solutions won't work, particularly those that put more taxpayer money into helping people buy more private health insurance. Private health insurance is not only extremely costly; it will also result in more and more *under*-insurance and will actually move us *away* from achieving quality universal coverage. In order to maintain profits and control their costs, private insurers will jack up deductibles and co-pays and cut benefits. Private insurers will do all they can to recruit the healthy and avoid the sick, who are burdened with pre-existing conditions.

That's the fallacy of the "level the playing field" argument put forward by politicians and pundits who propose that we offer Medicare to everyone and let it compete with private health insurance. The competition will not be fair, because private insurers will figure out how to attract the well by offering perks like free health-club memberships and by advertising aggressively among healthier groups, and how to skip over the less healthy by undermarketing to high-risk populations, even if they are legally required to insure all applicants. This will inevitably leave a disproportionate number of the sick to Medicare, which will in turn raise Medicare premiums, which will make it less attractive to healthy people than private insurance.

Many reformers advocate regulating private insurance to prevent these abuses, but the record of government regulation in this country is poor. The private industry being regulated uses its clout to constrain and distort government intervention. Moreover, no one has proposed comprehensive regulations to curb the worst features of the insurance industry, its built-in desire to avoid paying claims. Most regulation being proposed primarily involves selling insurance, not actually paying for health care.

We already have a clear example of how private health insurance avoids regulation when it coexists with public health insurance when we compare traditional Medicare to Medicare Advantage in which private insurance companies provide coverage. These private plans receive 12 to 18 percent more funding than traditional Medicare and yet have been fraught with major problems. "Tens of thousands of Medicare recipients have been victims of deceptive sales tactics and had claims improperly denied by private insurers according to a review of 91 audit reports conducted by the New York Times."[12] The companies reviewed included three of the largest participants in the Medicare market, United Health, Humana, and Wellpoint. The problems, described in the audit reports, include "the improper termination of coverage for people with H.I.V. and AIDS, huge backlogs of claims and complaints, and a failure to answer telephone calls from consumers, doctors and drugstores. . . . The audits document widespread violations of patients' rights and consumer protection standards. Some violations could directly affect the health of patients—for example, by delaying access to urgently needed medications."

The danger of halfway solutions is not only that they won't work but also that their failure can discredit the whole effort on behalf of universal coverage. The public will blame the advocates for universal coverage for the lack of improvement in affordability and coverage. Moreover, the halfway measures that have been proposed add legitimacy and resources to the private insurance companies, who will use those assets to fight single payer every step of the way.

The movement for single-payer National Health Insurance in the United States must come from the bottom up, and by the power of our numbers must bring enough politicians over to our side. It won't be easy, given the array of forces that will oppose it. But political outcomes are never determined only by the wishes of powerful elites. And some of the elites (e.g., businesses outside the health insurance and pharmaceutical industries) could potentially be moved by a determined popular movement and by the unwillingness of their employees to accept the growing restrictions and cutbacks on coverage that are generally the preferred response of business.

Building a powerful movement will require a creative combination of activism and education about how the public can start to make their government respond to the needs of ordinary people. It will be a challenge, but the only alternative to a single-payer system is to consign the people of our country to a more and more brutal health care system. The single-payer movement not only can win a humane health care system but also can contribute, in the words of Michael Moore, to making the United States more of a "we" society than a "me" society, one in which the individual and the society can truly flourish.

Health care is an essential safeguard of human life and dignity, and there is an obligation for society to ensure that every person be able to realize this right.

—Joseph Cardinal Bernardin

If access to health care is considered a human right, who is considered human enough to have that right?

—Paul Farmer

Afterword

James Winkler

It sometimes seems to me there are two ways of looking at the world. Either you believe we are all in this together and we need to care for one another or you feel that life is nasty, brutish, and short and you can rely only on yourself, your family, and those like you.

In a moral society, we are all in this together. In a moral society, everyone has a right to health care. The tragedy—and the promise—of America at the turn of the twenty-first century is that both ways of looking at the world have strong proponents. Fifty years ago, despite Congress's failure to legislate national health care, there were understandings of moral behavior to one another that were largely shared by the broad American public. Hence the subsequent advances in civil rights and the rights of women.

In the interim, powerful ideological forces have not only captured significant arenas of national leadership, but through their control of the corporate world have also promoted an ideology characterized by few rights and their

James Winkler is the General Secretary of the General Board of Church and Society.

corresponding social responsibilities. Whether one names this ideology neoconservatism or social Darwinism, at its heart it is alien to American ideals, because in its admiration for the individual who with little assistance from others achieves material success, it looks on the person in need—whether through poverty, misfortune, or disease—as being intrinsically undeserving.

In a moral America, health care would be a right. In a moral America, we are all in this together. A government-managed single-payer financing system is the only credible means by which the entire population can have equitable health care.

The idea that we're all in this together is not new to America and it is not new to the world. In the wake of the horror of World War II, many countries of the world decided that we needed to stand together and protect and care for one another. The Universal Declaration of Human Rights, adopted by the United Nations in 1948, declares, in part, "Everyone has the right to a standard of living adequate for the health and well-being of himself and his (*sic*) family, including food, clothing, housing and medical care and necessary social services, and the right to security in the event of unemployment, sickness, disability, widowhood, old age or other lack of livelihood in circumstances beyond his control."

The failure of the health care system in today's America to meet the universal ideals intrinsic to human rights and religious morality extends beyond the injustice of unequal access and taints even the nature of the care that is delivered. The provision of health care in America has been subverted from a calling to a commodity measured in patient encounters, tests performed, medications dispensed, beds filled, and above all, to profits distributed to the CEOs and stockholders of hospital corporations, pharmaceutical giants, and health insurance conglomerates. In the process, quality of care suffers as the primary consideration is often cost, not care.

The physician-patient relationship has been perverted, transformed from a caring relationship into a series of billable events. The physician-patient relationship is thereby compromised not only by the physician's motivation to sell the greatest number of services, but also by the motivation of insurance companies to pay for as few such services as possible. It has been estimated that today's physician spends about one third of his or her time satisfying insurance company regulations and seeking approvals for treatment, time the physician could be spending with patients. Managed care companies, HMOs, PPOs, and the like interfere with the physician's ability to develop comprehensive treatment plans for his or her patients.

High premiums force people to choose between health insurance and sustenance, housing, or other needs of a family, making even basic health insurance too expensive for an average individual or family. More than half of all personal bankruptcies are now the result of illness. Even individuals with ostensibly good insurance, let alone those who are uninsured, find themselves in situations where they must sell or spend all assets, including homes, in order to qualify for Medicaid and restore any medical coverage at all.

Several years ago, I was in Norway for a conference. One evening, I walked back to the hotel with a Norwegian. He said to me, "If you slip and fall and break your head open, our nation will care for you as we do for our own people. But if it were to happen to you or me in your own country, we would have to prove we have private health insurance just in order to receive medical assistance. Tell me, what is wrong with you people?"

What is wrong is that we are failing the test of social responsibility. There is something wrong with a society that has the means to provide health care for its entire people but refuses to do so. Dr. Martin Luther King Jr. warned, "A nation that continues year after year to spend more money on military defense than on programs of social uplift is approaching spiritual doom." These many years later, tens of millions of Americans do not have health care coverage.

The great religions of the world affirm that all people are connected to one another, that nature must be sustained and cared for, and that the conditions for a good life must be provided by society. Those in power in the United States, however, promote an "ownership society" that thinly veils the notion that all rights belong to the well-off and none belong to those who find they have nothing.

Civil and human rights have never come without a struggle. In most developed countries, the struggle for health care coverage has been won. Health care is recognized as a societal responsibility. The fight continues in the United States because of the power of greed. However, the insurance companies have overreached, their greed results in misery and suffering and causes millions of Americans to suffer terribly, and thousands to die prematurely.

A single-payer health care system will entitle all persons within the borders of the United States to the provision of health care services, the cost of such services to be equally shared by taxpayers and the government and distributed to providers in a coordinated, comprehensive, and equitable manner.

We really are all in this together.

Notes

1. It's good for our health

1. S. Dorn, *Uninsured and Dying Because of It: Updating the Institute of Medicine Analysis on the Impact of Uninsurance on Mortality* (Washington, DC: Urban Institute, 2008).

2. E. Nolte and C.M. McKee, "Measuring the Health of Nations: Updating an Earlier Analysis," *Health Affairs* 27 (2008): 58–71.

3. CNN.com, "Doctor Contrasts His Cancer Care with Uninsured Patient Who Died" (April 11, 2007).

4. D. Grady, "2 New Approaches May Reduce Cervical Cancer Deaths for Poor," *New York Times,* November 2, 2005.

5. Organisation for Economic Cooperation and Development, *OECD Health Data 2007*. (Paris: OECD, 2007).

6. Save the Children, *State of the World's Mothers 2006: Saving the Lives of Mothers and Newborns* (Westport, CT: Save the Children, 2006).

7. K. Hill et al., "Estimates of Maternal Mortality Worldwide Between 1990 and 2005: An Assessment of Available Data," *Lancet* 370 (October 16, 2007): 1311–19.

8. *OECD Health Data 2007*.

9. L. Payer, *Medicine and Culture* (New York: Holt, 1996).

10. M. Roemer, *National Health Care Systems of the World, Vol. 1* (Oxford and New York: Oxford University Press, 1991).

11. A. Shimo, "The rise of private health care in Canada," *MacLean's,* April 25, 2006.

12. Washington Post/ABC News Poll, October 20, 2003; Community Service Society/Lake Research, "Unheard Third," Question 11, 2007.

13. E. Smollett, personal communication, 2003.

14. L. Towell and S. Corbett, "Patients Without Borders," *New York Times Sunday Magazine,* November 18, 2007, 62–69.

2. It costs less and saves money (unlike all of the alternatives)

1. Kaiser Family Foundation and Health Research and Educational Trust (HRET), *2007 Kaiser/HRET Employer Health Benefits Survey.* www.kff.org/insurance/7672/upload/Summary -of-findings-EHBS-2007.pdf (accessed September 11, 2007).

2. U.S. Department of Commerce, Bureau of the Census, *Income, Poverty, and Health Insurance Coverage in the United States: 2006* (Washington, DC, August 2007).

3. Aaron Catlin et al., "National Health Spending in 2006: A Year of Change for Prescription Drugs," *Health Affairs* 27, no.1 (2008): 14–29.

4. Organisation for Economic Cooperation and Development, *OECD Health Data 2007* (Paris: OECD, 2007).

5. Ibid., and Commonwealth Fund, *National Scorecard on US Health System Performance* (New York, 2006).

6. Robert J. Blendon et al., "The Public Versus the World Health Organization on Health System Performance," *Health Affairs* 20 (2001): 3.

7. It is often claimed that Switzerland and, since 2006, the Netherlands rely on private insurance companies, as we do. It is true that these countries use private, including for-profit and nonprofit, insurance companies, but they operate under the most stringent government regulation. They must all offer the same standard benefit package, their premiums are regulated, and individuals pay according to their income, with government subsidy covering the rest. The government performs risk adjustment among the insurers, so there is no incentive for them to select only the healthiest persons and, in Switzerland, they are not permitted to earn a profit on the basic package of benefits.

8. John Holahan, *The Cost of Care for the Uninsured* (Washington, DC: Urban Institute, November 2005).

9. At $4,500 per person for the 47 million uninsured, private insurance would cost $212 billion. However, there would be less uncompensated care, and the Urban Institute study (ibid.) extrapolated to this year suggests that eliminating this and other costs paid for the uninsured would save about $60 billion.

10. www.ama-assn.org/amednews/2006/03/06/bisd0306.htm (accessed October 24, 2007).

11. S. Woolhandler, T. Campbell, and D. Himmelstein, "Costs of Health Care Administration in the United States and Canada," *New England Journal of Medicine* 349 (2003): 8.

12. James G. Kahn et al., "The Cost of Health Insurance Administration in California: Estimates for Insurers, Physicians, and Hospitals," *Health Affairs* 24 (2005): 6.

13. http://www.timesunion.com/AspStories/storyprint.asp ?StoryID=635848 (accessed October 24, 2007).

14. See www.pnhp.org/facts/single_payer_system_cost.php for a summary.

15. *2007 Kaiser/HRET Employer Health Benefits Survey*.

16. *OECD Health Data 2007*.

17. The VA Hospital system should not be confused with hospitals operated by the U.S. Army such as the Walter Reed Army Medical Center, which has been the subject of recent negative press coverage because of substandard care for returning troops.

18. Philip Longman, *The Best Care Anywhere: Why VA Health Care Is Better Than Yours* (Sausalito, CA: PoliPointPress, 2007).

19. www.house.gov/conyers/news_hr676_2.htm (accessed November 27, 2007).

20. The Lewin Group, *Health Care for All Californians Act: Cost and Economic Impacts Analysis* (Falls Church: January 19, 2005).

3. It will assure high-quality health care for all Americans, rich or poor

1. S. Dorn, *Uninsured and Dying Because of It: Updating the Institute of Medicine Analysis on the Impact of Uninsurance on Mortality* (Washington, D.C.: Urban Institute, 2008).

2. E. Nolte and C.M. McKee, (2008). "Measuring the Health of Nations: Updating an Earlier Analysis," *Health Affairs* 27 (2008): 58–71.

3. Kevin Sack, "Cancer Society Focuses Its Ads on the Uninsured," *New York Times*, August 31, 2007.

4. *Future of Emergency Care* report, Hospital-Based Emergency Care: At the Breaking Point, Institute of Medicine, June 2006.

4. It's the best choice—morally and economically

1. Douglas Fraser, "Inside the 'Monolith'," in *The State of the Unions*, ed. George Strauss, Daniel G. Gallagher, and Jack Fiorito (Madison, WI: Industrial Relations Research Association, 1991), p. 413.

2. Ricardo Alonso-Zaldivar, "Q & A: A Labor Leader Talks Healthcare," latimes.com, March 11, 2007, http://www.latimes.com/business/careers/work/la-na-unionqampa11mar11,1,2339035,print.story?ctrack=1&cset=true (accessed April 4, 2007).

3. For an elaboration of some of the main arguments in this chapter, see Marie Gottschalk, "Back to the Future? Health Benefits, Organized Labor, and Universal Health Care," *Journal of Health Politics, Policy and Law* 32, no. 5 (December 2007): 923–70.

4. For more details on organized labor and the battle over the Clinton plan and on the development of private-sector health benefits, see Marie Gottschalk, *The Shadow Welfare State: Labor, Business and the Politics of Health Care in the United States* (Ithaca: Cornell University Press, 2000).

5. Comments made at "A Brookings Institution–New American Foundation Forum: Employment-Based Health Insurance: A Prominent Past, But Does It Have a Future?" Washington, DC, June 16, 2006, http://www.brookings.edu/comm/events/20060616.htm (accessed July 18, 2006), p. 15.

6. George Raine, "Union Leader Declares Health Care Is Priority," *San Francisco Chronicle*, November 4, 2006.

7. "A Brookings Institution–New America Foundation Forum," p. 9.

8. Uwe E. Reinhardt, "Health Care Spending and American Competitiveness," *Health Affairs*, Winter 1989: 5–20. See also Mark Pauly, *Health Benefits at Work: An Economic and Political Analysis of Employment-Based Health Insurance* (Ann Arbor: University of Michigan, 1997).

9. See Gottschalk, "Back to the Future," pp. 946–47, Figures 1 and 2.

10. Steven Greenhouse and David Leonhardt, "Real Wages Fail

to Match a Rise in Productivity," *New York Times*, August 28, 2006, p. A-1.

11. Clifford J. Levy, "The New Corporate Outsourcing," *New York Times*, January 29, 2006, sec. 4, p. 1.

12. Pauly, *Health Benefits at Work*, p. 119.

13. Joe Nocera, "Resolving to Reimagine Health Costs," *New York Times*, November 18, 2006, p. C-1.

14. Cathy A. Cowan et al., "Burden of Health Care Costs: Business, Households, and Governments, 1987–2000," *Health Care Financing Review* 23: 3 (Spring 2002): Table 1, p. 136.

15. Cowan et al., "Burden of Health Care Costs," p. 132.

16. For details of the unraveling of the private-sector benefits, see Gottschalk, "Back to the Future?" pp. 926–40.

17. Ellen E. Schultz, "Companies Sue Union Retirees to Cut Promised Health Benefits," *Wall Street Journal*, November 10, 2004, p. A-1.

18. Chris L. Peterson and Rachel Burton, "U.S. Health Care Spending: Comparison with Other OECD Countries" (Washington, DC: Congressional Research Service, September 17, 2007), p. 1.

19. Uwe E. Reinhardt, Peter S. Hussey, and Gerard F. Anderson, "U.S. Health Care Spending in an International Context: Why Is U.S. Spending So High, and Can We Afford It?" *Health Affairs* 23, no. 3 (May/June 2004): 14, Exhibit 2.

20. Robert J. Blendon, Minah Kim, and John M. Benson, "The Public Versus the World Health Organization on Health System Performance," *Health Affairs* 20, no. 3 (May/June 2001): 16, Exhibit 1.

21. Henry J. Aaron, "The Cost of Health Care Administration in the United States and Canada—Questionable Answers to a Questionable Question," *New England Journal of Medicine* 349, no. 8 (August 21, 2003): 801.

22. Philip Mattera, "Taking the Profit Out of Health Insurance," *New Labor Forum* 16, no. 3–4 (Fall 2007): 51.

23. Ibid.

24. David U. Himmelstein, Steffie Woolhandler, and Sidney M. Wolfe, "Administrative Waste in the U.S. Health Care System in 2003: The Cost to the Nation, the States, and the District of Columbia, with State-Specific Estimates of Potential Savings," *International Journal of Health Services* 34, no. 1 (2004): 79–86.

25. Calculated from Himmelstein et al., p. 79.

26. John R. Commons, *Institutional Economics: Its Place in Political Economy,* vol. 2 (Madison: University of Wisconsin, 1961 [1934]).

27. Comments made at "A Brookings Institution–New America Foundation Forum," p. 15. The S.E.I.U.'s Web site also proclaims, "It's Time for an American Solution to Our Health Care Crisis." See http://www.S.E.I.U..org/issues/american_solution.cfm (accessed August 9, 2006); and Alonso-Zaldivar, "Q & A."

28. See, for example, Robin Toner and Janet Elder, "Most Support U.S. Guarantee of Health Care," *New York Times*, March 2, 2007, p. A-1.

29. Paul Krugman, "Big Table Fantasies," *New York Times*, December 17, 2007.

6. It will let doctors and nurses focus on patients, not paperwork

1. J. Needleman et al., "Nurse-staffing Levels and the Quality of Care in Hospitals," *New England Journal of Medicine* 346, no. 22 (2002): 1715–21; K. Chang, "Dimensions and Indicators of Patients' Perceived Nursing Care Quality in the Hospital Setting," *Journal of Nursing Care Quality* 11, no. 6 (1997): 26–37.

2. R.L. Kane et al., *Nurse Staffing and Quality of Patient Care*, AHRQ Publication No. 07-E005 (Washington, DC: U.S. Department of Health and Human Services, 2007); National Academy of Science, *Keeping Patients Safe: Transforming the Work Environment of Nurses* (2004). Retrieved December 23, 2007, from http://www.nap.edu/openbook/0309090679/html/18.html.

3. L.H. Aiken et al., "Hospital Nurse Staffing and Patient Mortality, Nurse Burnout, and Job Dissatisfaction," *Journal of the American Medical Association* 288, no. 16 (2002): 1987–93.

4. Bodenheimer and Grumbach, *Understanding Health Policy* 4th ed. (New York: McGraw-Hill Medical, 2004).

5. H.J. Keeler and M.E. Cramer, "A Policy Analysis of Federal Registered Nurses Safe Staffing Legislation," *Journal of Nurse Administrators* 37, no. 7/8 (2007): 350–56.

6. Needleman et al., "Nurse Staffing Levels."

7. Aiken et al., "Hospital Nurse Staffing."

8. Keeler and Cramer, "A Policy Analysis."

9. Aiken et al., "Hospital Nurse Staffing."

10. Kane et al., "Nurse Staffing and Quality." California Nurses Association, *RN-to-Patient Ratios: A Cost Effective Solution for Hospitals* (2005). Retrieved December 23, 2007, from http://www.calnurses.org/assets/pdf/ratios/ratios_patient_safty.pdf.

11. U.S. Department of Labor, Bureau of Labor Statistics, *Registered Nurses* (29-1111.00). Retrieved December 23, 2007, from http://www.bls.gov.

12. New York City Department of Health and Mental Hygiene, Triennial Report, *2004–2006*, "Public Health in New York City," p. 24.

13. Ian Urbina, "In the Treatment of Diabetes, Success Often Does Not Pay," *New York Times*, January 11, 2006.

7. It will reduce health care disparities

1. Centers for Disease Control and Prevention, National Center for Health Statistics, *National Linked Files of Live Births and Infant Deaths*, 2004, http://www.cdc.gov/nchs/linked.htm.

2. C.C. Cowie et al., "Prevalence of Diabetes and Impaired Fasting Glucose in Adults in the U.S. Population: National Health and Nutrition Examination Survey 1999–2002," *Diabetes Care* 29 (2006): 1263–68.

3. A.K. Jha et al., "Racial Trends in the Use of Major Procedures among the Elderly," *New England Journal of Medicine* 353 (2005): 683–91.

4. Agency for Healthcare Research and Quality, *National Healthcare Disparities Report, 2006*, http://www.ahrq.gov/qual/nhdr06/nhdr06.htm.

5. C. DeNavas-Walt, B.D. Proctor, and C.H. Lee, U.S. Bureau of the Census, *Current Population Reports*, P60-231, "Income, Poverty, and Health Insurance Coverage in the United States: 2005" (Washington, DC: U.S. Government Printing Office, 2006).

6. U.S. Department of Commerce, Bureau of the Census, Table HI-4, "Health Insurance Coverage Status and Type of Coverage by State All People: 1987 to 2005," http://www.census.gov/hhes/www/hlthins/historic/index.htm.

7. N. Calman et al., *Separate and Unequal: Medical Apartheid in New York City* (Bronx Health REACH Coalition, 2005), http://www.institute2000.org/policy/medical_apartheid.pdf.

8. It will eliminate medical debt

1. U.S. Department of Health and Human Services, Centers for Medicare and Medicaid Services, Office of the Actuary, *National Health Expenditure Data*.

2. Families USA; see *Kaiser Daily Health Report*, "Health Insurance Premium Rates Increase Faster Than Income, Study Says," October 18, 2006. The study examined premium growth from 2000 to 2006.

3. U.S. Department of Commerce, Bureau of the Census, "Income, Poverty, and Health Insurance Coverage in the United States: 2006," August 2007.

4. Paul Fronstin, "Sources of Health Insurance and Characteristics of the Uninsured: Analysis of the March 2006 Current Population Survey," Issue Brief No. 298, Employee Benefit Research Institute (EBRI), October 2006.

5. Mercer Human Resources Consulting, "2005 National Survey of Employer-Sponsored Health Plans," see Tab 4 at http://www .dppl.com/Mercer_Bos_2006/. Also see Paul Fronstin and Sara R. Collins, "Early Experience with High-Deductible and Consumer-Driven Health Plans: Findings from the EBRI/Commonwealth Fund Consumerism in Health Care Survey," EBRI and the Commonwealth Fund, Issue Brief No. 288, December 2005.

6. Kaiser Family Foundation/Health Research Educational Trust, "Employer Health Benefits 2007 Annual Survey," September 2007.

7. Jessica Banthin, Peter Cunningham, and Didem Bernard, "Financial Burden of Health Care, 2001–2004," *Health Affairs* 27, no. 1, 188–95 (Jan/Feb 2008).

8. Michelle M. Doty, Jennifer N. Edwards, and Alyssa L. Holmgren, "Seeing Red: Americans Driven into Debt by Medical Bills: Results from a National Survey," The Commonwealth Fund, August 2005.

9. ABC News, Kaiser Family Foundation, and USA Today, "Health Care in America 2006 Survey," October 2006.

10. See The Access Project, "The Consequences of Medical Debt: Evidence from Three Communities," February 2003; David

U. Himmelstein et al. "Illness and Injury as Contributors to Bankruptcy," Health Affairs Web Exclusive, February 2, 2005; Jessica H. May and Peter J. Cunningham, "Tough Tradeoffs: Medical Bills, Family Finances and Access to Care," Center for Studying Health System Change, Issue Brief No. 85, June 2004; and Michelle M. Doty, Jennifer N. Edwards, and Alyssa L. Holmgren, "Seeing Red: Americans Driven into Debt by Medical Bills: Results from a National Survey," The Commonwealth Fund, August 2005.

11. Catherine Hoffman, Diane Rowland, and Elizabeth C. Hamel, "Medical Debt and Access to Health Care," Washington, DC: Kaiser Commission on Medicaid and the Uninsured, September 2005.

12. Himmelstein et al. "Illness and Injury." content .healthaffairs.org/cgi/content/full/hlthaff.w5.63/DC1.

13. Robert W. Seifert, "Home Sick: How Medical Debt Undermines Housing Security," Boston: The Access Project, November 2005.

14. Brian Grow and Robert Berner, "Fresh Pain for the Uninsured: As Doctors and Hospitals Turn to GE, Citigroup, and Smaller Rivals to Finance Patient Care, the Sick Pay Much More," *Business Week*, November 21, 2007.

15. Cindy Zeldin and Mark Rukavina, "Borrowing to Stay Healthy: How Credit Card Debt Is Related to Medical Expenses," New York: Demos and The Access Project, January 2007.

16. Carol Pryor, Andrew Cohen, and Jeffrey Prottas, "The Illusion of Coverage: How Health Insurance Fails People When They Get Sick," Boston: The Access Project, 2007.

17. Kaiser Family Foundation and Health Research and Educational Trust, *Employer Health Benefits: 2006 Annual Survey*, 2006. www.kff.org/insurance/7527/.

18. See the Institute of Medicine, "Consequences of Uninsurance" series, several reports issued between 2001 and 2004. www.iom.edu/?ID=4660.

19. Healthcare ARM Report, Rockville: Kaulkin Ginsberg, 2006.

9. It will be good for labor and for business

1. *Consumer Reports*, September 2007, 16–18.

2. Ibid.

3. Ibid.

4. U.S. Department of Commerce, Bureau of the Census, *Income, Poverty, and Health Insurance Coverage in the United States: 2006* (Washington, DC, August 2007).

5. U.S. Department of Health and Human Services, *Health United States 2007* (Washington, DC, November 2007).

6. Kaiser Family Foundation and Health Research and Education Trust, *Survey of Employer Health Benefits 2007*, September 2007.

7. Alan Sager, "Hospital Closings and Consolidations Won't Promote Sustainable Health Care for All in New York," Testimony before the Workers' Rights Board, Buffalo, New York, January 30, 2007.

10. It's what most Americans want—and we can make it happen

1. Organisation for Economic Cooperation and Development, *OECD Health Data 2007* (Paris, 2007).

2. U.S. General Accounting Office, *Canadian Health Insurance: Lessons for the United States* (Washington, DC: June 1991); U.S. Congressional Budget Office, *Estimates of Health Care Proposals from the 102nd Congress* (Washington, DC: July 1993).

3. C. Schoen et al., "Why Not the Best: Results from a National Scorecard on Health System Performance," Commonwealth Fund Commission on a High Performance Health System, New York, September 2006.

4. "Toward Higher-Performance Health Systems: Adults' Health Care Experiences in Seven Countries, 2007," Health Affairs Web Exclusive Vol. 26, No. 6, p. w717, Exhibit 4.

5. L. Kowalczyk, "Dangerous Delays to see Skin Doctors," *Boston Globe*, January 7, 2007.

6. Richard Roetzheim et al., "Effects of Health Insurance and Race on Early Detection of Cancer," *Journal of the National Cancer Institute* 91, no. 16, (1999): 1409–15.

7. Kevin Sack, "Cancer Society Focuses Its Ads on The Uninsured," *New York Times*, September 7, 2007.

8. S. Dorn, *Uninsured and Dying Because of It: Updating the Institute of Medicine Analysis on the Impact of Uninsurance on Mortality* (Washington, DC: Urban Institute, 2008).

9. D. McCormick, D. Himmelstein, and S. Woolhandler, "Single-Payer National Health Insurance: Physicians' Views [in Massachusetts]", *Archives of Int Med* 164 (2004):300–304.

10. American College of Physicians, Position Paper: "Achieving a High-Performance Health Care System with Universal Access: What the United States Can Learn from Other Countries," *Ann of Intern Med.* 148 (2008):55–75.

11. www.kff.org/kaiserpolls/pomr101606pkg.cfm.

12. Robert Pear, "Medicare Audits Show Problems in Private Plans," *New York Times*, September 2, 2007.

THIS MODERN WORLD

by TOM TOMORROW

Between the health care that we now have and the health care that we could have lies not just a gap, but a chasm.

—*Crossing the Quality Chasm*

Resources

National Organizations and Campaigns

Physicians for a National Health Program
http://www.pnhp.org
> 29 E. Madison, Suite 602
> Chicago, IL 60602
> Phone: (312) 782-6006
> Fax: (312) 782-6007
> PNHP's 15,000 members across the United States advocate for a universal, single-payer national health program. The Web site provides a wealth of information and resources. (You don't have to be an MD to join.)

All Unions Committee for Single Payer Health Care—HR 676
http://unionsforsinglepayerhr676.org
> c/o Nurses Professional Organization (NPO)
> 1169 Eastern Parkway, Suite 2218
> Louisville, KY 40217
> Phone: (502) 636-1551
> A clearinghouse rather than an organization, this is where to find the names of the 400 local and international unions, state

labor federations, and Central Labor Councils across the United States that have endorsed HR 676.

American Medical Student Association (AMSA)
http://www.amsa.org
AMSA, with a half-century history of medical student activism, is the oldest and largest independent association of physicians-in-training in the United States. AMSA is a leading organization that works to rally students for national health care.

Healthcare-NOW!
http://www.Healthcare-NOW.org
Healthcare-NOW! is a national campaign for a quality guaranteed nonprofit single-payer health care system in the United States.

Latinos for National Health Insurance (LNHI)
http://www.latinos.nhi.org
LNHI is a national coalition working for equality in health care. LNHI's mission is to educate Latino organizations, individuals, government officials, and community leaders about the need to establish a comprehensive, universal, equitable, and affordable program of national health insurance in which everyone is covered from birth.

National Health Care for the Homeless Council
http://www.nhchc.org
The National Health Care for the Homeless Council is a membership organization that works to improve access to health care, quality of care, and health status of homeless people as part of the broader struggle to end homelessness.

National Nurses Organizing Committee (NNOC)
http://www.calnurses.org/nnoc/about-nnoc.html

> The NNOC is a new national union and professional organization for Registered Nurses, Advance Practice Nurses, and RN organizations throughout the country who want to pursue a more powerful agenda—including getting national, guaranteed health care for life in the United States. One of the fastest-growing health care organizations in the United States, the NNOC presently has 80,000 members in 50 states.

SiCKOCure.org
http://www.SickoCure.org

> SiCKOCure.org was set up for those who have seen the movie *SiCKO* and want to learn more about what they can do. It is a project of PNHP, California Nurses Association/NNOC, and HealthCare-NOW!

State and Local Organizations

California Nurses Association (CNA)
http://www.calnurses.org

> The CNA, and its national arm, the NNOC (see above), is one of the nation's premier nurses' organizations and health care unions.

Everybody In, Nobody Out
http://www.everybodyinnobodyout.org

> Everybody In, Nobody Out supports state organizations working at the grassroots for universal health care.

OneCareNow.org grassroots campaign
http://www.onecarenow.org
> OneCareNow is a 365-city program to educate millions of Californians and build massive support for passage of universal health care (SB 840) in California.

Single Payer Now!
http://singlepayernow.net
> Single Payer Now! is a grassroots association of volunteers supporting Universal Single Payer Healthcare for California since 1994.

Consumer Watchdog
consumerwatchdog.org
> Consumer Watchdog is a California group that fights to protect patients, to improve the quality of health care, and to create universal health care.

New Yorkers for Single Payer Healthcare
http://www.hungeractionnys.org/

Research and Policy Resources

Commonwealth Fund
http://www.commonwealthfund.org
> The Commonwealth Fund is a private foundation that supports independent research on health care issues and offers grants to improve health care practice and policy.

Consumers Union (CU)
http://www.consumersunion.org

CU is an expert, independent, nonprofit organization whose mission is to work for a fair, just, and safe marketplace for all consumers.

Dēmos
http://www.demos.org

Dēmos is a nonpartisan public policy research and advocacy organization that focuses on four areas: democracy reform, expanding economic opportunity, restoring trust in a government by and for the people, and promoting new ideas in the public debate.

Families USA
http://www.familiesusa.org

Families USA is a national nonprofit, nonpartisan organization working at the national, state, and community levels and dedicated to the achievement of high-quality, affordable health care for all Americans.

General Board of Church & Society (GBCS)
http://www.umc-gbcs.org

GBCS is the international public policy and social justice agency of the United Methodist Church. GBCS advocates for health care for all in the United States by focusing on a single-payer national health plan on the state and federal levels, protecting the building blocks of universal health care (Medicare, Medicaid, Veterans Health, Indian Health Service, and employer-sponsored health care insurance), and promoting the Health Care Justice Sabbath Program.

Guaranteed Healthcare
http://www.guaranteedhealthcare.org

Guaranteed Healthcare is an action page dedicated to getting the United States National Health Insurance Act passed. You can write your representative, sign up for action alerts, communicate with the press, and tell your own story about the American medical system.

Health Affairs
http://www.healthaffairs.org

Health Affairs is the leading journal of health policy thought and research. Published since 1981, the journal is nonpartisan and presents a wide range of timely research and commentary on health issues of current concern in both domestic and international spheres. All articles *Health Affairs* has published are available online.

Kaiser Family Foundation
http://www.kff.org

A leader in health policy and communications, the Kaiser Family Foundation is a nonprofit, private operating foundation focusing on the major health care issues facing the United States, with a growing role in global health. Unlike grant-making foundations, Kaiser develops and runs its own research and communications programs, sometimes in partnership with other nonprofit research organizations or major media companies.

Medicare Rights Center (MRC)
http://www.medicarerights.org/

MRC is the largest independent source of health care information and assistance in the United States for people with Medicare. Founded in 1989, MRC helps older adults and people with disabilities get good, affordable health care.

Public Citizen Health Research Group

www.citizen.org

Public Citizen is a national, nonprofit consumer advocacy organization founded in 1971 to represent consumer interests in Congress, the executive branch, and the courts.

About the Contributors

Olveen Carrasquillo, MD, MPH, is an Associate Professor of Medicine, Health Policy and Community Partnerships at Columbia University Medical Center. He is also the Director of the Columbia Center for the Health of Urban Minorities. His areas of research include minority health, health disparities, health insurance, and access to care.

Representative John Conyers Jr., a Detroit Democrat, was re-elected to the 14th Congressional District in November 2006, to his twenty-first term in the U.S. House of Representatives. For more than three decades, Congressman Conyers has led efforts in Congress to reform the health care system. He is the founder and chairman of the Congressional Universal Health Care Task Force.

Rose Ann DeMoro is the Executive Director of the California Nurses Association/National Nurses Organizing Committee, AFL-CIO, which, with 80,000 members, is the nation's largest union of direct-care RNs. DeMoro has been honored by *MSN* as one of the most influential women of 2006, in *Esquire's* Best and Brightest issue, and as one of the 100 most influential persons in health care by *Modern Healthcare* for several years running.

Claudia M. Fegan, MD, is the Associate Chief Medical Officer for the Ambulatory and Community Health Network for the Cook County Bureau of Health Services and the former President of Physicians for a National Health Program. The daughter of a labor union organizer and a social worker, Fegan received her undergraduate degree from Fisk University and MD from the University of Illinois College of Medicine.

Oliver Fein, MD, is a practicing general internist, Professor of Clinical Medicine and Public Health, and Associate Dean at the Weill Cornell Medical College. He is Vice President of the American Public Health Association, Chair of the New York Metro Chapter of Physicians for a National Health Program (PNHP) and President-elect of National PNHP.

Leo W. Gerard is International President of the United Steelworkers and is the son of a nickel miner. As an eleven-year-old, he listened to union meetings held by his father in the basement of the family home. They instilled basic social democratic values and union principles and led to a lifelong commitment to social change and justice.

Marie Gottschalk, PhD, is a professor of political science at the University of Pennsylvania. A former journalist and editor, she is the author of, among other works, *The Shadow Welfare State: Labor, Business, and the Politics of Health Care in the United States* (Cornell, 2000) and *The Prison and the Gallows: The Politics of Mass Incarceration in America* (Cambridge, 2006).

Joanne Landy, MPH, MA, is the former executive director of the New York Metro Chapter of Physicians for a National Health Program. In addition to working on health care issues, Landy is co-director of the Campaign for Peace and Democracy.

Martha Livingston, PhD, is Associate Professor of Health and Society at the State University of New York College at Old Westbury. She is Vice-Chair of the Board of Directors of the New York Metro chapter of Physicians for a National Health Program.

Mary E. O'Brien, MD, is a primary care internist at Columbia University Health Services and a faculty member at the Columbia College of Physicians and Surgeons. She is on the Board of Directors of the New York Metro chapter of Physicians for a National Health Program and is the chair of its media committee.

Leonard Rodberg, PhD, is Professor and Chair of the Urban Studies Department at Queens College/CUNY, where he teaches health policy and other urban issues. He was one of the founders of Physicians for a National Health Program and now serves as Research Director of the NY Metro Chapter of PNHP.

Mark Rukavina is the Executive Director of the Access Project, which focuses on promoting health access at the local community level. He oversees all programs designed to assist communities in their efforts to address the health care access issue. He is responsible for developing strategies and community linkages with state and national health policy administrators.

Jaime Torres, DPM, MS, is the founder and president of Latinos for National Health Insurance, a national coalition of Latino leaders advocating for national health insurance. He is also an Associate at the Aesthetic Realism Foundation in New York and was on the Advisory Board of the National Hispanic Medical Association.

Nathan Wilkes is an entrepreneur and devoted father, currently living with his wife and three children outside Denver, Colorado. When not working, he often lectures on patient advocacy and emergency preparedness. Wilkes is currently on the boards of Health Care for All Colorado and the National Business Coalition for Health Care Reform.

James Winkler is the General Secretary of the General Board of Church and Society, the social justice and public policy advocacy agency of the eight-million-member United Methodist Church. The board is headquartered on Capitol Hill in Washington, DC in the historic United Methodist Building and works to secure health care for all people.

Cindy Zeldin is a health policy researcher with nearly a decade of public policy experience at the state and national levels. She is currently pursuing a PhD in Health Services Research and Health Policy at Emory University.

Acknowledgments

First and foremost, we would like to thank Ellen Adler for inviting us to write this book. We are tremendously grateful to her and to Jyothi Natarajan of The New Press both for the opportunity and for their generous help and advice.

Were it not for the twenty-year fight for a single-payer health program waged by Physicians for a National Health Program (PNHP), this volume would not have been written. We owe an enormous debt of gratitude to Oliver Fein, Joanne Landy, and Len Rodberg. In addition to their having contributed two of the chapters, they helped shape the book overall, identified potential contributors, and read and gave wonderful suggestions on much of the manuscript. Susan Moscou did a terrific edit of one of the chapters. Thanks to Steve Auerbach, Laura Boylan, Michelle Desanno, Debbie Feuerman, Elaine Fox, Ida Hellander, Robert Padgug, Carol Schneebaum, Betsy Todd, and Nick Unger for their guidance, research help, and suggestions. Thanks, too, to Stephen Kirkpatrick and the rest of the fabulous librarians at SUNY College at Old Westbury.

Many thanks to all of our contributors for their hard work and dedication to the movement for health care justice.

Martha would like to thank Roger Bellin, Carla Livingston, Samantha Livingston, Freddy Thomas, Jude Thomas, Ed Livingston, Chris Kennedy, Bill Livant, Diana Ralph, Anne Hunter, Suzanne Curley, Karen Palmer, and Freda Steinberger for their help, unfailing love, and support. Martha would like to honor the memory of Mila Rainof, who would have been a wonderful doctor.

Mary thanks John Gorman, a thoughtful reader and editor of every chapter, and her sons, Nick and Patrick, for their frank feedback on content and the design of the book from a younger generation's perspective. Finally, Mary thanks the thousands of patients she has treated over the past thirty years. It is they who compelled her to recognize that guaranteed and universal health care is indeed a human right.

Despite the best efforts of those we acknowledge above, the responsibility for any errors in the manuscript is ours alone.